vocation questions & answers

vocation
questions & answers

Fr Anthony Bannon, LC

CIRCLE PRESS
Hamden, CT

CONTENTS

To the man who, on my first visit
to the seminary to see if I had a vocation,
pointed upwards and said, 'He's the one who calls.
Ask him, offer yourself to him,'
and has never ceased to show me
what it is to be a priest.

INTRODUCTION

A vocation is a mystery.

How does a vocation come about, how does it become clear, what obligations does it bring, what are the implications of taking it, or of leaving it...? Like unwanted guests the questions batter at our door, while inside all we want is some calm and peace.

As always when there is mystery afoot, our reason and understanding are a little uncomfortable. They know they have a job to do—namely, to figure things out—but they also sense that they might not be quite up to this one, for they are faced with something that goes beyond their control, something too big for everyday categories.

This book is the result of questions and answers on vocations asked over the Internet by real people I do not know personally. Certain themes recur, and the real-life situations are vivid in a way no position paper could ever be. The answers of course are centered on the particular questions, and any spiritual or theological points made are precisely and solely to enlighten the particular question raised. I have tried to be as practical as possible.

For this book I took the themes most often inquired about and tried to give them some order with a certain continuity and complementarity. My divisions may be somewhat arbitrary and a certain amount of repetition was unavoidable, but I hope this does not take away from the fruit to be gained from reflecting on the themes.

The space given to certain topics reflects not so much their relative importance in the abstract, as their practical importance and urgency for the greater number of those who asked the questions. However, I think that on the whole there emerges a rather complete picture that can be of use to you.

Sometimes I provide a link between one question and the following, but mostly they are freestanding, and you don't have to read them in any particular order.

Though many questions were made anonymously or under obvious pseudonyms, I have opted to rename all the inquirers. I edited out unnecessary parts of the questions, and I have kept other editing to the minimum. However, I considered it in your best interest that I polish up many of my answers.

I hope you enjoy this book and find something helpful here.

CHAPTER ONE

The Nature of Vocation

THE FUNDAMENTAL MYSTERY

Before tackling others' questions it may help to ask one ourselves: Why does Jesus say that we should *pray to the Lord of the harvest that he send laborers into his vineyard?*

On first impression it does not make sense: from before they were born God knows those he wants to call, and we presume he intends to do so, so there doesn't seem much for us to do there. And the person called has to respond freely, so it seems that here too we are limited to being spectators. Maybe he really meant to say that we should pray that those called will be generous? But he said *pray... that he send...* Obviously he is telling us that our prayer will make a difference.

It must also mean that a vocation, though it comes from God, does not become a reality in someone who remains totally passive.

Vocations are not only to pray for if we like, a nice and proper thing to do. We must pray for them if they are to happen. A vocation is not only something that happens to you; it is something you have to take and make happen if God seems to point that way. It is important to keep this in the back of your mind as a point of reference for what follows.

---

the mystery of God in your life

Theresa asks a disarmingly simple question that is a springboard for much deeper reflection.

Why should I think about becoming a priest, sister or brother? What are the highlights of becoming a priest, sister or brother? What would I get out of it?

Dear Theresa,

If the thought has come into your mind it is always a good idea to take time to think about it further. I think the first step to do this is not so much to engage in a specific investigation into the vocation itself, but rather to go to something much deeper and much more basic.

You should think about why you were given the gift of life and where your life is going.

In order to do this you need to use your faith, because our faith tells us things about our lives and this world that we cannot discover without it, very important things. Faith also makes us sure about things we would not otherwise know for certain. That means that when we think about our lives we do not do so in a vacuum, or at the mercy of the confusing variety of opinions we hear around us and see portrayed on TV, or the experiences and opinions we personally have.

Faith lets us know that we are more than just our bodies and our feelings. It gives a purpose and meaning to what we do. It gives us something to strive for, helps us understand the problem of pain and suffering, satisfies our mind, helps us understand what love is and how fundamental it is, and it is a constant among so many changeables in our lives.

Then, don't just think about these things, talk to God about them. Pray. At times we think prayer is either feeling, or saying words by heart. These can come into prayer, but we also need to use our head in prayer and think as we talk to God. There are some basic convictions that a life of faith brings into our lives that guide our actions and choices; when we pray it comes home to us that God is everything, nothing outside of him is worth much. God loves us, he has saved us, he has prepared and won eternal life for us. Our present life only has meaning when compared with eternal life, and eternal life is something we don't gain by default, we do have to do something with the help of his grace to get there. This something consists in our love for others, our service to others in our attempt to be like Christ.

So then the vocation to priesthood, brotherhood or sisterhood becomes much more important than 'what is in it for me?' understood in a material sense like 'what will I get out of it here and now'; it does answer 'what is in it for me' when we take into account what is most important when you have a Christian view of life: how can I love and serve God the best, get to live with him eternally, and help others get there too. It means 'what does he want me to do with my life?'

How do you go about discerning what God's plan for you is?

Dear Paul,

The shortest questions sometimes need the longest answers, but at the risk of being sketchy I will try to zero in on the important points that can get you started.

The first thing to do is to live the present moment – in a good sense and not in the 'carpe diem' mode. God will always make himself present to you where he expects to find you. You are baptized, so he will expect to find you working to overcome sin and develop your life of grace. He plans to meet you in the sacraments (confession, Eucharist), and in prayer. He has given you his Mother as yours and so will look for you close to her. As well as being baptized you have other duties and obligations (as a student, at home...). He has given you human qualities and abilities: He expects you to be working on them. If you live up to what is expected of you, you are more likely to be able to hear his voice.

The second thing is to trust God. He will not play games with you. Seek with absolute trust.

The next crucial thing is to be ready to say Yes to whatever God wants of you. As far as I can see, this is the major part of discernment. The main problem is not in being able to see what God wants, but in not being willing to do it. Then try to take it a step further: Tell

Christ to use you whatever way he wants; offer yourself to do the most difficult work for him. Don't worry, it is not easy to do this so don't be alarmed if at first you cannot say the words.

The next steps build on the above. Look around. See what God has done for you. See where he has led you. See the thoughts he has put in your heart. As well as the many attractive things you can do with your life, are there other desires in your heart such as the desire to serve him, to save souls, etc.? Follow up on those. Look specifically into your vocation by doing a retreat, visiting places you are interested in, getting a spiritual director.

And look at the practical side: If you have debts to take care of, studies to make up, etc.

And all the time continue to pray and offer yourself.

---

a vocation takes work too

What can I do to learn about the priesthood? One more question: How do you know if you have a calling to become a priest or brother?

Dear Joe,

To learn more about the priesthood you can read Pope John Paul's story of his own vocation and his personal reflections on the priesthood in his book, *Gift and Mystery*. See if you can get a hold of Fulton J. Sheen's book (sometimes hard to find) called *Those Mysterious Priests*. Any well-done 'life of Christ' (again I recommend the one written by Fulton J. Sheen) will help you understand the call to the priesthood.

To know if you have a calling to become a priest or brother you have to look into it. Get advice from a good priest you know. It is a very good sign that you are even asking yourself the question, but you need the help of someone who knows you to be able to tell. Or visit a seminary or order that interests you; they will be able to help you.

---

women priests?

My roommate and I have been having lots of discussions about Catholicism, which I know is good, because it causes me to often ask why. Of late, we have begun discussing the role of men and women in the Church. Why is it that we believe only men can be priests? We talk about vocations, and following God's will. What if God's will for a certain woman is for her to become a priest? Could it be possible that this desire expressed by some Catholic nuns is a result of God's hand? Are there any Biblical references? Has this been an issue in the history of the church before? Thanks!

Dear Julie,

I am glad to hear you are asking questions about your faith; make sure you look for the answers in the right places so that the result is that you grow and mature in your faith. Get hold of a copy of the Catechism of the Catholic Church (you should be able to find it in any Catholic bookstore) and look up any point you want to discuss in it. As regards women and the priesthood, I will give you the short answer, and tell you where you can read more.

First of all, you have to remember that Jesus, even during his life on earth, was God as well as man, so he wasn't culturally limited as we are. He was a Jew, from a people chosen by God and receivers of special favors and care by him; they were the ones to whom God began to reveal himself. Now Judaism was different from the contemporary pagan religions in many things; among the differences was the fact that the Jews did not have priestesses. Jesus rose above many of the social taboos of the Jews of his time as regards his dealings with women, but he did not make any move to change the Jewish approach to priesthood. He chose twelve men as his apostles, ordained them, promised them the Holy Spirit would come, and guaranteed that he would be with them always.

Then you look at the history of the Church and you see that, contrary to all the propaganda out there, Christianity (and therefore Catholicism) has been the greatest uplifter of woman in history. The type of dedication St Paul tells a man to have for his wife (be prepared to give your life for her, like Christ did for the Church) was unknown up till then. The prominence of women, the influence of women saints, schools for women, etc... are all products of Christianity.

Why then no women priests? It would seem to be a logical progression, right? The answer is that Christ clearly didn't and doesn't want it.

Being a priest is not a matter of us wanting it; it is not a right you can invoke. I have dealt with many men who wanted to be priests that I have had to tell they can't. A further point that has a direct bearing on women and the priesthood is the identification between Christ and the priest, and the fact that the best title for a priest is 'father.'

As a summary, read also what the Catechism says in numbers 1577 and 1578. A more extensive explanation is to be found in the declaration *On the question of the admission of women to the ministerial priesthood* (its Latin name is *Inter insigniores*) published by the Sacred Congregation for the Doctrine of the Faith on October 15, 1976. You should be able to find it on the Vatican's website. You will find more in the document *On Priestly Ordination* (in Latin called *Ordinatio sacerdotalis*) by John Paul II, published on May 29, 1994, also available on the Vatican website. This document also shows how it is not a question of discrimination.

I hope this provides you with material enough to read and reflect. You will see that the train of thought is very well-reasoned, and the conclusions are, well, conclusive. Not something that you can change without rejecting all the way back to Christ himself. God bless.

---

can your vocation change?

What I was wondering was: If God has a specific vocation for you when you are born, does that vocation never change no matter what life you lead? What I'm trying to say is: Throughout your life is your vocation always the same, or does it change as you make different choices through life? Or on the other hand, can you have two and God gives you a choice between either one? Thank you.

Dear Anita,

Your question is quite speculative, but there are things that God tells us in Scripture that can help us as we try to answer it.

The best place to start may be to ask ourselves again what 'vocation' means. *Before you were conceived in your mother's womb I set you aside* (Jer 1:5). This is God telling us that he had something in mind for us when he gave us the gift of life, or rather even from before he gave us the gift. Something he wants us to be, and something he wants us to do. This is God's plan.

'Vocation' means 'call.' This means that as we grow up and develop, and especially as we approach the age at which we make major choices in our life, God offers his plan for us as a call. God would like me to be a priest, so he calls me to be a priest. He would like someone else to be a missionary, so he calls him to the missionary life. How do we hear him calling us? In prayer, in our personal experience, in the circumstances of life as they develop around us, in the needs we see that people have..., these are all ways to discover God's voice inviting, calling us to be and do something specific. God doesn't appear to us, but he calls us through these signs. It is he who is there behind them, nevertheless.

Does our vocation change? If our vocation is God's original plan for our lives then no, it cannot change; there will always be one thing that God made us for. What does change? My understanding of that plan can. I can join a religious order because God seems to be calling me, but a year or two down the line he might through various signs (not my feelings alone) show me his real plan is something else. The opposite happens too. Many young men who join the seminary thought for many years that they were called to marriage, lived good lives and went to college, until one day they finally saw that God was really pointing them somewhere else and accepted it...

Now, what happens if you have a vocation—let's say to religious life, you're pretty sure—but for whatever reason you choose something else, not something bad, but a good Catholic marriage with a good man? It won't be what God originally planned—there is no way to change that—but he is merciful not vengeful. He is not going to figure out some way to get back at you. As long as you do not close your heart to him, he will give you in the sacrament of marriage all the graces you need to live it well and live up to what God wants from married Christians. He is merciful and wants us to be saved, and even after our worst faults, as long as we turn to him, he forgives us, raises us up, and makes us capable of doing good things in his grace. In that sense perhaps you could talk about a 'second vocation.' The first one will always be in God's mind as his original plan, but if we go elsewhere he never stops calling us to holiness and to our real home, heaven. Just remember that following Christ, whether in your 'first' or 'second' vocation, will always mean entering by the narrow gate, so you can't talk about an 'easier' vocation.

---

would it be wrong for me to get married?

Here is a long letter, well worth reading through. It addresses a fundamental question, and even though we will dedicate a chapter to the question of marriage and celibacy, the answer goes well with our topic now, which is to attempt to understand what a vocation really is:

Hi, I am discerning a call to the priesthood. I am not sure if this is my vocation, but I have strongly felt it at times, even to the point of tears. I have also had people tell me that I may have a vocation (religious). I have ended up at very strangely 'coincidental' discussions about vocations.... I felt that God told me to look at both marriage and priesthood for the next 2 years (I am a junior in high school) and not close my mind to either one.

I was really having a hard time with this because I had met this girl that I really liked and it almost made me feel that it was pointless to talk to her... Then I read a scripture passage (1 Corinthians 7, especially verse 6) which led me to believe that I should really put my heart into discerning priesthood and not worry about marriage, because I could get married if I decide that priesthood isn't for me.

I have asked several people the following question and I always got short, confusing answers: If God calls me to the priesthood do I have to become an ordained priest? Would it be wrong for me to get married? Would I be less blessed as a married man? I know that it is better to be single for the sake of the Kingdom and not be pulled in two directions, and even now I really find a kind of freedom in not having any established 'relationships' with women, but part of me really wants to have a family... to pray family rosaries with a wife and kids... to work through the difficulties of marriage... to share every part of my life and myself with someone else... But I want to serve God and minister also... I long to share the Good News with people and feel that I would make a good priest... yet I long for marriage as well...

Sometimes I have gotten the impression that priesthood is an invitation and that it's up to me how I respond to it and that God will bless me either way, and sometimes I have gotten the impression that priesthood is a calling that I must respond to by discerning and becoming a priest... I really need some clarification here. I love God with all that I am, and will subject myself to his will even if it hurts, but do I have to become a priest if that is my calling?

Please help me with this. (I do, however, feel that I am bound to discern this, and find whether I have this vocation or not, but does any of this discernment go beyond, 'Does God want me to be a priest?' and into, 'Do I want to be a priest?'... Marriage is beautiful and I know that my admiration for marriage would make becoming a priest an even more beautiful sacrifice and that marriage is only temporary, but I really long for it.)

Am I running from God? Is my attraction to marriage merely a natural feeling outside of God's will for me? I have several friends who are also discerning the priesthood and they tell me that the only thing that attracts them to marriage is the sex, but for me the sex isn't even an issue. Thank you for reading this long and repetitive letter. I really need some clarification, though I don't expect you to be able to answer all my questions perfectly. Please help me out.

Dear Bruce,

You ask a very important question that goes to the heart of what a vocation is, what our freedom is, and how God treats us.

If you can, read George Weigel's book on Pope John Paul II called *Witness to Hope*. On pages 68-70, you will find a brief description of how the Pope as a young man came to understand he had a vocation, what his thoughts were, and how he answered and overcame the initial objections of some people who loved him dearly but tried to dissuade him from the priesthood. I think you will find those pages helpful.

The word 'vocation' comes from the Latin 'to call.' It is God who calls. When we discover a vocation, we discover that God seems to be inviting us to a closer relationship and service, as St Paul explains in the letter you mention. Since original sin has weakened our will and clouded our understanding, we find it very hard to understand God, for his call always seems to ask us to do something more difficult, almost impossible, and not what comes easier to us. For example: you realize what it is to be baptized, and by that fact you also realize that you cannot keep living like those who aren't; you have a commitment to live up to, a call to live up to—just read the Sermon on the Mount (Chapter 5-7 of Matthew)—even though at times it might feel like too much.

Now, some things God asks us to do are right in themselves, and not to do them would always be wrong – like forgiving. It is right to forgive, wrong not to, and that applies to everyone.

Other things God would like us to do, but not to do them would not in itself be something wrong – for example, being a priest. It is not wrong not to be a priest – if it were, very few men could be saved, and no women at all! It is only wrong for someone who is called to be a priest not to become one. But it is a different kind of wrong than the 'wrongness' of not forgiving. I hope you can follow what I am saying.

The outcome is this: a man who does not forgive has to reverse course if he wants God to forgive him, but if a man who is called to be a priest says No, and gets married, he has disappointed God because he has said No to him. However, if he is sorry, and asks God to forgive him, God will surely do so, not withhold his blessings, and offer him all the means to live a holy and fruitful life as a married man. He does not have to get unmarried and become a priest for God to forgive and help him. Got it?

When we perceive a vocation we may feel 'forced' but it is not the overpowering force of a God who says 'If you don't do what I say, I'll condemn you for it.' It is, rather, the force of love. If God has chosen us out of many to bring us closer to him in a special way, making us servants of his people to take away their sins and make Jesus present in a real way in their lives through the Eucharist, it is a great privilege and dignity, but also a great responsibility, for God has placed much hope and many lives in our hands.

When you look at it with eyes of faith, there is really only one answer to give, no matter what the cost. When you look at it with eyes of hope, there is only one answer, despite our weakness. When you look on it with eyes of love, there is only one answer, despite everything else that attracts us.

The greatest gift God gave us is the ability to love. Freedom is a gift that God gave us so we could love. Understanding and faith are gifts he gave us so we could spend our love on something worthy of it, something that will take us beyond this life and make us happy for all eternity. Reason and faith free us from appearances and our limitations so that we can give ourselves fully to God, the greatest good there is, and in that way use the gift of these years of life he has given us here on earth in the most fruitful and beautiful way possible. Doing what he would like us to do.

CHAPTER TWO

*Solving the Vocation Shortage,
Encouraging Others*

THE VOCATION SHORTAGE

what does the future hold?

I have a few questions to ask you. There is a lot of talk of how there is a shortage of vocations in the United States. How do you feel about this? Do you think that there is anything we as Catholics can do to help the numbers increase, or help those who think they have a vocation? Also, do you think that this is like a cycle and there will be a booming number of vocations in the future?

Dear Marian,

It is painfully true that the numbers of priests, seminarians and religious in the U.S. have dropped. Not everywhere, since there are some dioceses that now have more vocations than ever, but in general despite a recent upswing we are not at former levels. And all the while, the number of Catholics has grown.

This has led people to all sorts of conclusions, some of which border on the bizarre. Some speak about the problem in purely sociological terms: There are fewer people available to do more work so the future holds the promise of nothing but increased pressure, reorganization and redistribution of personnel, while a harried, overworked clergy fight an unwinnable battle. Their answers to the problem are also mainly sociological: change the rules so priesthood will be more attractive and we'll get more. Others figure that since God is in charge, the vocation shortage is his doing; this means he is leading us to a 'less clerical' future in which Providence has pegged the priest as a vanishing breed to make laypeople come into their own. So for them the problem needs no further solution; it's a non-problem, it's the way to go.

Here is an alternative line of thought:

The lack of clergy has acted as a trigger, making many laypeople wake up to their baptismal privilege and responsibility: every baptized person partakes of the priestly, prophetic and kingly mission of Jesus Christ. The new breath of the Holy Spirit in the Church, inspiring an astounding variety of lay movements and apostolates, has come just at the right time. As a result more laypeople are taking personal responsibility for the Church, and doing much of what they expected Father or Sister to do in the past. Their reaction is no longer 'the Church should do something about that' but 'I have to do something'.

Is this awakened sense of the layperson's call to holiness and apostolate the death knell for clergy? Does an active laity mean we need fewer priests? Quite the contrary. We need more, since priesthood is service, not privilege. A lax Catholic needs a priest only occasionally, perhaps Mass every other Sunday, confession only rarely... while a fervent, active Catholic will seek Mass even daily, feel the need for reconciliation frequently, and being educated he will seek reasons and answers, look for spiritual direction, advice, support, instruction.

An active Catholic will also seek the support of those who dedicate their whole lives to prayer, the contemplatives. He will have a sense of the communion and complementarity that exists among the different vocations in the Church, and will see that the Church needs those who live for God alone, to the exclusion of everything else. He will pray that God will enrich the Church, and help him as a layperson by calling many to the priesthood.

For its part, this increased fervor of the laypeople—especially of the young—and the changes it means in their lives and their families will itself foster vocations. The better we follow Christ, the more we will pray for vocations and the more there will be, since God will answer those prayers he has inspired in us. When a local Church is fervent, God always blesses it with souls who consecrate their whole lives to him: as priests, nuns, consecrated laypeople, contemplatives.

So to increase vocations, the first and most important thing we can do is to try to live a holy and active Christian life and pray for the vocations we need. But, we must also work to foster them. Here are some things to do. One, if you are young, ask yourself if he might not be calling you. Two, if you know someone who might have a vocation, pick a good moment and tell him so. Three, do everything you can to help young people learn about their faith and practice it. Four, do everything you can to help young people avoid the damaging experiences many may meet when growing up, and prepare them to be strong in the face of those that cannot be avoided. This applies especially if you are a parent.

---

roots of the vocation shortage?

I believe that our priest shortage is a direct result of contraception. Could it be that God punishes us for that sin (it is known that Catholics contracept at the same rate as Protestants)? Why don't we hear more of these issues from the pulpit? It seems many priests are fearful of teaching the truth from the pulpit lest the numbers of parishioners decline. Wouldn't it be better to have a smaller number of Catholics and yet a larger percentage practicing truth than what we have now, which is a smaller number of priests teaching a larger number of so-called Catholics and a greater percentage of Catholics living a lie.

Dear Joan,

You have put your finger on a real problem. However, if we are going reflect on it, we must remember what we discover about God in Christ: the only 'punishment' God gives us for our sins is to send Christ to redeem us. So, rather than picture God actively punishing us for this sin, it would be more accurate to picture the loving Father (who did everything for us, creating us and sending his Son to redeem us) shaking his head in sadness as we leave the source of living water and try to slake our thirst in the cracked cisterns of our cultural desert. It just won't work; we won't find there what we need. It hurts him to see us try it, over and over again, despite the painful consequences.

The usual connection made between the contraceptive mentality and a drop in vocations is this: it makes for fewer children; therefore parents are less willing to give up one for God. You will often hear people toss in here as well the reflection that with increased affluence, parents no longer have to send sons off to the seminary to make ends meet. A very poor explanation.

We have to remember that God's ordinary plan for the believing Catholic is that he receive his faith and the living example of how to live it, from his parents. A vocation is in most cases a great blessing and reward that God gives to a family, a wonderful seal of approval on the Christian marriage of select parents (though not every saintly couple is blessed with a vocation in the family). For that reason a couple that engage in any practice that they know is wrong are not in a position to pass on to their children the real essence of our faith, which is loving obedience and trust in God. They are not giving God his place. They pass on to their children a skewed vision of reality and the faith, mostly self-centered. I think that is the real problem.

Here we see again that a vocation is not something that comes solely from on high, independently of our actions. God has an active part he wants us to play in fostering vocations. It is our responsibility. Our faith is a living reality: not so much a question of words, but of how we make our lives conform to those words... There is the challenge.

Is preaching from the pulpit the answer? Partially. Not, however, a preaching that issues from the letter of the law, but rather from the priest's personal experience of God, his personal fidelity to God, and his own integrity as a follower of Christ. That is what will give him the strength to preach this 'hard teaching' and what will move the hearts of those who listen to him.

---

it's no vocation pie

I am a high school seminarian considering the priesthood. I feel as if God may be calling me to serve as a missionary, especially in Latin America, but then I see the shortage of priests in our own country and I wonder whether if I should stay to help out here. Do you think I could still be possibly called to Latin America? If so how can I best prepare myself?

Dear Tom,

Jesus told his disciples not to fear, that he would be with them always. One of the reasons may be because no one of us can meet every need and solve every problem, much as he might want to. The needs of souls are overwhelming and no single person can work out what he needs to do, so the most intelligent course of action is to let God do the figuring and the choosing, and for us to follow his lead because we trust him. The Church and the world are in his hands; he is THE Good Shepherd.

Since we are limited, what we leave undone will always be more than what we do. No individual can serve everywhere and solve all the problems. Each is limited to what one person can do, and there is no way of escaping this reality.

If you feel God is calling you to be a priest in your home diocese, who is going to tend the sick, or pray and do penance in the monasteries, or go on the missions? Simply someone else that God is calling. If you are called to the missions in Latin America, who is going to take care of your diocese at home? Again, someone else that God is calling. If you are called to one diocese, who is going to serve him in the others? Once more, someone else that God is calling.

So look at where he is leading you, what he is putting in your heart, and be confident that if you are faithful to him, he will take care of the other concerns you have.

There is an underlying question here. Some people think there is just one, limited 'vocation pie' out there, so the bigger the slice that goes to the missions, the smaller the slice left for the home dioceses. Nothing could be more untrue. God loves everyone and is calling enough priests for everyone. He needs your example to inspire others. If he wants you for Latin America or somewhere else, I can guarantee you that your generosity, example and prayers are going to inspire others to be generous with him and follow their call. If God is calling you to the missions, the best way you can help your home diocese is by going on the missions, even if that seems a paradox. A diocese that does not contribute missionaries to spread the Gospel afar is not really alive. If you are called to the missions, you are God's way to give a truly missionary, service-oriented face to your home diocese.

ENCOURAGING OTHERS

---

my friend might have a vocation

I think my friend has a vocation because he wants to learn Latin and possibly would like go to a monastery over the summer. Also he is a great leader and when people say bad words he always tells them to not say them again. He likes to listen to good Catholic music. So how could I encourage him more to follow up on a vocation that a lot of people think he has?

Dear John,

I had a friend too that I used to think should be a priest, certainly not me, and things did not turn out quite that way. Maybe it will be different for you and your friend, so here are some suggestions (a lot depends, of course, on how close you are as friends and how frank you can be with him).

1. Pray for him. Pray that both you and he will be generous enough to do whatever it is God wants of each of you. This thought that has come into your mind is God's hint for you to give serious consideration to what he wants you to do with your life. You know that the Church is Christ's Mystical Body, and the health of each member affects all the others. Here is one of its concrete applications: you don't make others holy by telling them to be holy, but first of all by striving to be holy yourself. It is the same if you want to help others with their vocation.

2. Mention it to him. Don't just think it, say it. You may well be the instrument that God needs to make him realize what is happening in his life.

3. Stick together and help each other. Create a circle of good friends, and as well as having fun together and keeping each other out of trouble, do some constructive things that will help others in some way (help the poor, teach younger kids the faith, help out some old folks now that summer is here and the grass is growing, help younger kids at summer camps...).

4. Invite him on a retreat with you so that you both can pray about your vocations.

I hope some of this helps, and I will say a prayer for both of you.

---

helping a vocation, encouraging the thought

Dear Father, I realize how much the Church needs vocations and I would like to encourage young people to listen for the Lord's call and follow it. I understand the 'why' of encouraging vocations, but I feel that I need to be formed in the 'how.' What can you tell me about what I can do to help in this area?

Dear Jean,

Please don't laugh at this, but I think the first thing you should ask yourself when wondering whether a young man might have a vocation is this: 'Would I love to have him as a son-in-law?' If he doesn't pass that initial screening, he most probably does not have a vocation!

You are looking for someone who is normal, healthy, upright, enjoyable, steady, intelligent, more an optimist than a pessimist, practicing his faith, at ease...

Then you have to remember that the vocation happens in one's soul, so be on the lookout for a greater degree or spiritual interest and sensitivity, a concern about others, willingness to sacrifice himself for others, what is important for him in life, etc.

The best way to help a potential vocation is to ask him if he ever considered it. If he did, depending on the person, you can push you luck and ask him if he thinks God may have put those thoughts into his mind. Another step would be to ask him what he would do if he knew for sure God was calling him. Then you can ask him if he would like to find out if God is in fact calling, and propose a visit to check it out. Of course you can't cover all those steps in one conversation, but they are a helpful guide in dealing with a possible vocation, and they are reflections he needs to make if he is going to solve the vocation question. I hope this helps.

YOUR CHILD'S VOCATION

---

nurturing a son's vocation

A wonderfully generous mother asks this:

I would be so happy if one of my sons decided to become a priest or my daughter to become a sister. Only my youngest seems open. How should I approach conversations about this topic with them? This son says, 'If I were to become a priest,' and I listen and encourage his thought process. What about the other two who are more closed? Does that mean they are not being called? Thanks.

Dear Rose,

Funny things can happen inside children. At times, the one who acts like he is not interested when you are preaching to the others is precisely the one who is really soaking it up.

As you teach your children to be open to God, it is important that, more than hear your words, they see your example. They are going to absorb your priorities from the thousand ways your reflect them during your day, and if your example is consistent, if you give reasons when they challenge you (those teen years that are coming if they aren't here yet), most probably they will in time make them their own.

So, be what you are supposed to be. Without being artificial about it let them see you pray, teach them to pray, teach them the example of Jesus, relate it to their lives. Direct and encourage everything that is good. Correct what is wrong. Weather their tantrums and stay fast and teach. Help them grow, according to their age, in their relationship with God and knowledge of their faith. Challenge them appropriately. Lives of the saints are a great source of inspiration for children (and not only children).

What you are really doing is preparing the ground, so that as soon as God begins to give them a hint of what he has in mind for them, they will be able to recognize and respond to the call; you want them to have principles of faith to guide them, love to move them, and strength of character to be able to do what might be difficult.

As regards fostering their vocation directly, do not push it on them, but do not be silent either. Answer questions; at times bring them up yourself, raise the possibility. It seems to me that what you are doing will be helpful to them.

---

helping, when God is already at work

I am writing to seek advice on how I can guide my child through her spiritual growth. I have only daughters. The twelve-year-old has expressed many times over the past few years that she will become a nun. I really do not think a child of twelve understands what this means (nor do I for that matter). However, she feels inspired by the life of Mother Teresa. She has a strong desire to belong to an order that specifically helps the poor. Again, I am not sure she really understands what it means to devote your life in such a way. My basic problem is I do not know how to nurture this. She seems to have developed this on her own without much influence by mom and dad. I am not sure if I should expose her to this kind of life at this early of an age. As a family, we pray together. We say a family rosary most Sunday evenings. We go to church weekly and all holy days of obligation. We confess our sins every month or so.... We are also caught up in the materialistic way of life. All three daughters live very comfortable lives.

I have been blessed with a very successful career and have been able to provide quite a luxurious way of life.... We like our stuff. I would welcome any advice you can give, especially along the lines of when is it time to expose her to life as a nun, what guidance I can give her and how can I nurture what may be a very real direction for my daughter?

Dear Bill,

Your letter reflects beautifully several mysterious aspects of the way God's grace can work in different souls. It is at work in a young soul (your daughter's) inspiring a clarity beyond her years, although perceived in the simplicity and innocence she is still living. It is also at work in your soul inspiring awe and respect for his action, a desire to support it, and also a clarity of your own about the encroaching place material things are taking in your life.

Before anything else, I think you have to ask yourself where God is leading you personally. You are fulfilling your normal obligations as a Catholic, yet you seem to sense that something may be missing. Whatever it is, God seems to be giving you a gentle prod to go further.

It is important for your daughter that you move ahead yourself. Your increased personal commitment will make you more sensitive to God's action and more perceptive in relation to what is most prudent for her.

To clarify some things: God can give the grace of seeing his call to anyone at any age. As a Catholic father, you are called to take care of her spiritual needs as you do the material, and protect her spiritual health as you do her physical. Just as you work to give your family all the material things they need and more, pray and increase your Christian life in order to gain for them the graces they need to know and love God more. You already give good example in the way you live your marriage. If she is called to be a nun, it is important that she have your example of what a truly Christian marriage is, and recognize the goodness of marriage coming from God and leading to him; this will be one of the greatest helps for her to understand the nature of her vocation to love God exclusively if she is called to be a nun.

Help and encourage her prayer life, her awareness of God's love. Give her the opportunities she needs to learn, expand her mind and develop her character; allow her to continue and even increase her works of service. Let her read about Mother Theresa if she is inclined in that direction. As she continues to grow through her adolescent years, make sure her understanding, character, heart and faith are nourished harmoniously. Personally, I do not think it is too early for her to see a little more closely what the life of the Sisters is like. Perhaps on a family trip to one of the cities where they have a convent you might visit them as a family, for example. But don't forget, develop your own spiritual life to better help your daughter.

---

how do I help my son?

Our son is 14 years old and will be entering high school in the fall. I am praying for God's will for his life, whether it be the priesthood or marriage. He thinks Mass is a bore but told me he prays and thinks this is enough. We read religious books together and just finished the biography of St Maximilian Kolbe. We want to encourage him to listen to God's call if it was to be to the priesthood, but he doesn't want to hear of it right now. I, as his mother, pray every day for him. What more can we do?

Dear Janine,

From your note, it seems you are doing two very important things to help your son discover God's will: you are praying with all your hearts, and you are putting him in touch with the heroes of our faith, the saints. You are also actively encouraging him, a third important point. I am pretty sure that also as his parents you are unconsciously giving him many unspoken messages of what true Christian life, marriage and love are. This, too, is very important whether his vocation is to priesthood or married life.

I know very little else about your circumstances, so let me mention some general points that may have some bearing on your situation. He is 14, in the middle of growing up. Self-assertion. Maybe he respects you but gets a hard time from his friends. Don't underestimate either the power of your example or the power of the pressures he may be getting from outside. Don't despair, but also keep a close eye on his friendships. It will probably take a lot of talking (and often firmness) to keep him clear of danger and prepare him so he does not get over-influenced by the behavior of others. So, if there is any way that you can get him involved in good, worthwhile, fun and constructive activities while you continue to build up his spiritual life, it would be well worth doing so. If you can get him involved in an adventuresome apostolate like door-to-door missions that will put him in touch with other kids of his age or older who are looking for what is right in life, it may help too. What he may need is the example of support of kids his own age or slightly older.

CHAPTER THREE

Discernment, the Constant Problem

INTRODUCTION

The following question may seem a rather unusual one to start with, but I think it brings out the impracticality of what sometimes we call 'spiritual discerning,' and the inadequacy of concentrating on discernment alone.

My nephew believes he is to marry and does penance (fasting, prayer, Mass, rosary) to know God's will and to have his prayer for a wife answered. He is close to giving up. What can I do to encourage him and is there a saint he can read about to help him? Also, where can he meet a good Catholic girl?

Dear Dan,

If your nephew is truly convinced that he is called to marry, then he should make sure that he goes about it in a similar way to a young man who thinks he is called to the priesthood. Surprised?

What I mean is, prayer will only get you so far. Prayer without our cooperation will not bear its full fruit.

Prayer purifies our will, makes us capable of knowing what we are supposed to do, strengthens our spirit to follow Christ rather than the world, stirs up love for God in our soul, etc. That is all hugely important, but nevertheless incomplete. So your nephew has to complete his side of the equation by developing a normal, healthy (in a Christian sense) social life for a single man of his age. Social life is not limited to dances and parties. It is involvement with others. Teaching CCD in the parish can be part of a normal social life. Helping in youth groups, volunteering to coach in the parochial school or in the township, participating in choir, drama clubs, sports clubs, service projects... Any of these and many more can be the way God wants to answer his prayer and have him meet that 'special person' he knows must be out there.

GENERAL PRINCIPLES OF DISCERNMENT

---

can I know for sure?

I had a dream that someone came up to me and said, 'You are a nun' and that was all they said. It has been on my mind for quite a very long time. Not just the dream but also my vocation. I want to become a nun more than anything in this world. I don't want to get married. That's for sure. How would I know if it's what God wants? I know in my heart that He's calling me but I want to be 100% sure.

Dear Amber,

Don't pay too much attention to the dream; it is not the important part of your message.

You want to be 100% sure, but that is not possible before you actually take the step or before you are accepted for final vows. Your question is a good one, however; it is good that you are not totally satisfied with 'knowing in your heart' that God is calling you. You sense it takes more than that for a vocation, because it could be just your emotions. So you are right in looking for something more.

Before we get into what this 'something more' could be, let me raise a word of caution. You say you know for sure you don't want to get married. Why you don't want to is important and has a bearing on your vocation. If you have nothing against marriage itself but only mean that you have already made up your mind it is not what God is asking of you, fine. But if you have something against marriage, or an aversion to it, you should definitely look into this, because it is not healthy or right. Such an aversion would certainly not be a sign in favor of a vocation, it would definitely be a sign against – at least until you overcome it.

Supposing your views on marriage are healthy and Christian, and you feel strongly in your heart that God is calling you to be a nun, there are a few steps you can take to be more sure and find out where.

One, keep praying.

Then, get a spiritual director and talk with him (or her) about the impediments to a vocation. If there are none, you can be a little surer of your vocation.

Let the spiritual director get to know you and judge if your attraction is more than emotion.

Examine how you are living your life now to see how you are doing as regards God's will for you where you are at present. If you are underage, do you obey your parents? If you are at college, do you stand up for your principles? Is there discipline in your life (any trouble with weight, anorexia, addictions)? If you are a student, do you study? Those sort of things. It is amazing how often we want to be saints, right on the top of the ladder, yet we never take the step onto the first rung. You are not going to be magically transformed when you join the convent, and if you live for yourself now and give in to your whims you will have a rough time then. The change will be too much. So test your vocation by being what you should be now.

Then you should also look into specific orders, and visit them. You need to do this to see if you really fit. Really fitting doesn't mean you do not find it difficult; it just means there is a sense of being at home there, an identification with the spirit you see in the nuns.

All of the above will help you confirm if what you are feeling in your heart is something that comes from God, and if you should act on it. Once you join, and then live the life to the full, you will be in a position to gain 100% certainty over time.

---

how do I begin the process?

I had a powerful experience at this past Easter Vigil, and I felt what I thought might be a tugging at my heart to join the sisterhood. This is not the first time this has happened. I've never been through a serious discernment process, but I have considered a vocation and even told the Lord I would do it if he wanted it that way. (Of course, it's been so long I'd probably have to do that again.) But at the time it seemed like I needed to finish out my degree and get started in the workforce. I have had much dating experience, but very little experience with serious relationships and have wondered if this could be a hint. My question is: How do I begin the discernment process and where should I go to find out about specific orders? There are so many, I just don't know whom to go to first. I love Mother Angelica and have daydreamed about what it would be like to be one of her sisters. But I have very little direction in this. Not to mention the town I live in is very small and I don't even know of any local orders. Please help.

Dear Louise,

A strong tug at our hearts might be a wake-up call, but it is not in itself the definitive sign of a vocation.

Your reaction, however, is the correct one – to check into it further especially if the thought has been recurring. You can do several things, some spiritual and some practical.

One, pray. But don't just say, 'God show me what you want and I'll go.' (Much less say, 'Show me what you want and I'll think about it.') Say something like, 'Lord, you gave me only one life to live, it is the only chance I have to do good and bear fruit. Use me. Whatever the cost, I want to live only for you.' You will have to pray that over and over in order to mean it.

Two, trust. You are not on an impossible quest. God is practical enough to make sure you come into contact with the place where he wants you to be.

Three, seek, in order to find. One thing you need to seek is someone who can be your spiritual advisor. It can be a priest or religious you trust. With this spiritual director you should talk in depth about your life up to now and your present situation, so that he (or she) can tell you if there are any signs that God is not calling you.

Four, seek the place to visit. There is already something about Mother Angelica's nuns that has attracted you. Start there. That may or may not be your call, but take the first step. If you visit them and it is not your path, they will put you onto some other possibilities. One thing at a time.

Five, don't expect everything to work out immediately. You will have to invest time; there will be difficulties and doubts – but we need all those for God to purify us so our love for him can grow.

---

crucial first step

How exactly does a man become a priest? What steps should be taken before entering the seminary?

Dear Daryl,

I am going to guess a little, and suppose that your question really is: If I think I have a vocation, what should I do?

The first thing to do is make a decision.

No matter what your age, if you think you might have a vocation, make the decision that you are going to follow it, no matter what. That is something you do in prayer, because it is a promise you are going to make to Christ.

Once you do that, then look at what your circumstances are so as to figure out what the concrete steps are going to be. These concrete steps will depend on circumstances such as your age, present obligations, possibilities, spiritual development, degree of knowledge as regards a vocation, etc.

Before entering the seminary, you have to get in touch with the vocations director and speak to him about your vocation and your circumstances, and get his advice. Once he gets to know you, he will be able to tell you if you show the signs of a vocation, and if it seems like the right time to apply, or if there is something you need to work on before you take a step into the seminary.

You will have to trust him and work with him.

---

attractions and distractions

I am 16 and a sophomore in high school. After I went on a retreat, I felt strongly about joining the religious life. Sometimes I feel very strongly about it, but when I am distracted by other things, like friends, or sports, or whatever else, I feel like I am not being called to the religious life. How do I keep from losing my attraction to the religious life, but still go on living my own life in the present time? How do I know that those feelings of joining the religious life are reliable, and if that's what I am really called to?

Dear Michelle,

I think the key to your situation can be found in the words you use. You 'felt strongly' about religious life, you 'get distracted' with other things which makes you 'feel like' you are not being called, and you want to make sure you don't 'lose your attraction' to the religious life.

What this means is that you are still at the first level of discovering your vocation and you now have to go deeper, otherwise you will never find stability or any real answer.

You have experienced a number of things. One is that our emotions and feelings can be helpful, they can push us towards something good. Second, you have experienced that emotions are fickle. Third, you have seen that emotions tend to be caused mostly by something that seems good and beneficial and we have right there in front of us. Our feelings usually go for the latest thing: you are on a retreat and you get enthusiastic about your vocation, you go to a game or a dance and you are attracted by something else, you go to a movie, and depending on what it was, you feel joyful or sad.

You ask how can you know if your feelings of joining the religious life are reliable, and the answer is they aren't. Surprised? On their own, they aren't reliable enough either for you to count on them lasting forever, or for you to base a life decision on them. They may be just the start, the first awakening of a vocation, but no more. Once they have got you thinking, you have to go beyond them, go much deeper.

The question you have to tackle now, and what is going to become the bedrock of your vocation if you have one is: Is God calling me to be a religious? Notice the big difference here: the question is not about your feelings but about what God wants. And remember that it is not unusual for what God wants to actually go against our feelings. No matter how much you feel like gossiping and adding in a few tidbits that are not exactly true but will ensure an avid audience, you should never give in and do what you feel like; a person who feels like getting drunk shouldn't just give in and follow the feeling; and if you are flooded with feelings of hate, envy, pride, etc., you don't want to give into them, you want to overcome them.

I hope this helps you to see what you are working through. The first thing you need to do now is start talking to Jesus about this in your prayer, especially when you go to Communion. Ask him 'What do you want me to do, what did you give me the gift of life for?'

---

when and how

I am a senior in high school. I have found a very good spiritual director. I am very attracted to the priesthood. I don't feel a very strong calling to marriage, although some of my best friends are women (girls). I am extremely attracted to the priestly grace-filled abilities of absolution and consecration (of the Eucharist). I will begin college in the fall. I'm planning on a major in psychology.... I am willing to go in full pursuit of a vocation to the priesthood. But, I'm afraid that doing so, I may become so focused that I miss heavenly hints to another vocation (marriage). And, I don't know much about priestly duties outside of Mass and offering sacraments. Or know much about all the different religious orders that exist. Should I go full steam ahead in a priestly pursuit, or take some time to learn more about the religious life before I dive in that direction? Thank you for your time.

Dear Kevin,

Your spiritual director is going to be able to give you much more pertinent advice since he knows you much better than I do.

Let me just tell you a general principle I go by. If you are interested in the priesthood, have the opportunity of following the call, and a prudent advisor does not see anything missing that you have to work on before being accepted into the seminary, then it is time to move, putting aside the other distractions and possibilities (there will always be dozens of other good things to do, so don't let that be the reason you do not follow your vocation).

For example: You mention that you don't feel a strong calling to marriage yet you get on well with women. But you are only finishing high school, and you are probably better off at this stage not feeling that strong call – because it often becomes strong precisely when there is somebody special in mind. So you can still be a normal teenager and not feel an overwhelming attraction to marriage at this stage of your life. But if a young person is unsure of his identity, and for that reason doesn't have the normal attraction to marriage, then this is something he would have to sort out before taking a step into the seminary.

Another point to keep in mind is that if you go to college you will in all likelihood start running up debts that will afterwards make it more difficult for you to enter a seminary.

It would be a very good idea for you to look into some religious order you may have heard of, and get the ball rolling. Early summer is a good time to do this, but make sure to enroll in college as well so as not to be caught in the fall without one or the other.

---

where do my wants come in?

I am 21 years of age and have always thought of becoming a priest. I met with my vocations director here in the diocese but I thought I would contact other priests just to get some opinions. I was just wondering how you know it is time to become a priest or how did you know you wanted to be a priest? I have thought about it a lot and came very close last year to joining our seminary but changed my mind the last second. I do not know if that was the sign to not pursue this or if I was just nervous. I always come back to priesthood though around this time and I cannot stop thinking about it. I do not know if this means that I want to be a priest or not. I am confused about what God wants and was hoping for an opinion you may have on this matter.

Dear Jeremy,

It does seem you have 'the vocation bug.' The fact that your thoughts about the vocation keep coming back means something, at a minimum, that it's an issue that you need to deal with more fully.

I think a good deal of the confusion you feel may be due to an incomplete understanding of what a vocation is, so here are some pointers.

One, a vocation is a call from God: we don't invent it, no one else can give us one; it can come only from him. The main question to be asked and answered when thoughts of the priesthood come into our mind is this: 'Does God want me to be a priest? Is he calling me?'

Two, if God calls us, then we have to answer something: basically either yes or no.

This is where my 'wanting' my vocation comes in. My 'wanting' it or 'being interested in it' does not make the vocation, but my wanting has to come into the picture, and this is where it comes in: 'Which do I want to say to God, Yes or No, if he is calling me?'

But that seems to beg the question, 'How can you say Yes or No if you are not sure he is in fact calling you?' So,

Three, there are some signs that are necessary for a vocation; it will help to look and see if they are present in your life.

Let us check the signs: you must have health enough for the vocation. This includes physical health (the minimum will vary according to different vocations), psychological health (free from major scars, neuroses, dependencies, for example – you are going to guide others so your own house has to be in order), and spiritual health (belief in the Church, practice of the sacraments, giving prayer a place in your life, etc.). You must also have the human maturity that corresponds to your age, and be able to take on commitments and function stably in your present responsibilities. There must be a core to you that is not overly influenced by others so that you live by principle rather than by others' opinions. And your motives for considering a vocation must come from your faith, and not from human convenience or gain.

Four, to go beyond the signs and actually discover if you have a vocation you need something else besides signs: you have to be 'on good terms with God,' you have to 'speak his language.'

What is God's language? Love. You can only get in a position to figure out if God is calling you if you love him, if you are struggling (though you might fall at times) to grow in your life of grace, doing good, avoiding sin, serving others, giving God time in prayer. And I think you can only open your soul to the vocation if you love people, and love them enough to give your life to serve them.

Five, 'abstract' vocations don't exist. God calls to something specific, either diocesan priesthood or some specific religious order. When you find the place God wants you to be, you usually have two contrary reactions: one is a sort of 'click,' a recognition, 'Yes, I fit; if I were to be a priest, this is the type of priest I would want to be.' And simultaneously I think there has got to be some fear, a recognition that this is not going to be easy, I'm going to have to give a lot, grow a lot, put myself in second place.

So, what do I suggest you do now? See if you have the initial signs. Then pray, saying to God: 'Maybe it's you who are putting these thought in my mind, inviting me. Help me to be generous enough if it is you, because you know there are lots of other things I would like to do as well.' Then look. Visit seminaries. Don't go on a wild spree, just start by visiting the ones you know, do a retreat with them, and see if that 'click' happens. At this point you will definitely need some outside help: You need to open yourself to the men who run that seminary or order where you have 'clicked' so that they can evaluate and give you their read on your situation vis-à-vis joining their group.

You may think I have avoided the part of your question that asks how you know it is time to become a priest. I haven't: You simply cannot know before you do all the above. If you have the general signs, find the right place, are accepted (or at least encouraged), and there are no substantial reasons to wait, it means 'now's the time.'

---

nun, where to start?

I think the Lord is calling on me to become a nun. I hear him but I'm not sure where to go to get questions answered. I haven't seen a nun in my area in years. Should I go to the archdiocese? Maybe I should move to Alabama and have Mother Angelica help me. That would be great!!!! Many Blessings and Love.

Dear Amy,

There are few details in your message, and to give concrete advice I would need more to go on (age, studies, responsibilities, spiritual interests, etc.), so let me just say some very general things.

Pray. Now that the thought has come into your mind, you have to take responsibility for it, to make sure it grows and bears fruit. Prayer is to spend time with God. Visit him in the Eucharist, go to Mass more often, speak to Mary and put your vocation in her hands. Don't ask so much for signs, as to get to know Christ so that he can transform you heart. 'Lord, help me love the things you love.' Spend time thanking him for all he has done for you.

Then, start moving (supposing of course that you are old enough, and there are no signs that God is not calling you). You mention the archdiocese. That is one way, but if you are given brochures and information on all the communities in the archdiocese, it may be confusing because of the sheer amount of information on different communities.

I find it much more helpful if you start off inquiring with groups you are already familiar with. You mention Mother Angelica. Without having to move to Alabama, you can ask her convent for information, possibly visit them sometime. Then work from there. Sooner or later you are going to hear of or meet a group that, for some strange reason you may not be able to explain completely, attracts you. Your heart pulls you back to them. Follow up on that one.

Most helpfully of all, if you don't have a spiritual director you should look for one. A good spiritual director will know something about religious orders and will also get to know you well and have a good idea where God's grace is leading you.

... I too have been discerning a vocation in the past year. I used to be really worried about it, but now I've figured that if that's God's plan for me, then it will happen. I don't have to decide today. I appreciate your telling Amy to pray that she may come to know and love Christ better. I am really taking that to heart as my course of action right now. I'm not afraid anymore that I might have a religious vocation. I know that if He wants it, it will be, and it will be great!

Dear Julie,

Thank you for your kind lines. As regards your own vocation – yes, focus on knowing and loving Christ better, but don't forget to do each day what he asks of you, to show him the love you want to have for him.

And don't wait for him to tell you what to do. As you get to really love him, you will start asking yourself, 'What would please him most?' When you love someone, you don't wait around to see if he asks you for a favor – you are always on the watch to see what he would like and surprise him with it, aren't you?

making things complicated

How do I know if my thinking about a vocation might not be a prideful thought?

Dear Jack,

The only way you can tell if your inclination towards a vocation is a prideful thought is by examining your conscience, because pride is in us as an attitude and disposition we have. But you are going to have to go beyond that to answer the vocation question, for there is a difference between our attitude and God's will, and knowing one does not determine the other. This is beginning to sound like a riddle so let me say it another way.

Your inclination towards a vocation may be a prideful thought, and yet God might still be calling you. You would simply be desiring the right thing for the wrong reason. Conversely, it is possible that God really is calling a person who is leaning away from a vocation out of false humility. Of course the trick is to do the right thing for the right reason. How do you do that? By trying to get to the bottom line of what a vocation is.

Vocation is what God is calling you to do. To answer a vocation properly, you have to put him, his will and his example, at the center. You may be proud and think you are worthy of the priesthood, or have great ambitions of future glory... but look at the priesthood of Christ: service, work, persecution, betrayal, death, and only afterwards the resurrection. Are you willing to follow him under those conditions? By praying and putting his example at the center you can purify yourself of your pride, or if you can't get rid of it completely (the most common case) you can at least curb it out of love for him.

DISCERNMENT: WHEN TO START

---

what happens if I'm seesawing?

Hi. How do you know when it is the right time to start discerning something? What do you do when one day you think that yes, it is the time, and then the next day you think maybe it isn't? Are you ever completely sure? Please help. Thanks for your time.

Dear Shannon,

It is OK at any age to ask if God is calling you to give your life to him. You can ask yourself the question even if there is no possibility of you doing it right away, and there is no urgency to it.

It is always good to get help from someone if you can when you are discerning. If you are at a stage in which you can take a step, then you really need to ask yourself the question and look for an answer.

It is very normal to have wide swings when we are discerning a vocation, because we often go on our feelings – one day we feel there is nothing we would like more than to be a priest or nun, and the next day all we want is a family, and maybe the day afterwards we don't feel even like taking on the responsibility of a family and just want to be free and have a good time.

That's why, even though we tend to make discernment a thing of our feelings, we should try to go much deeper. We have to make sure our discernment is really the attempt to get all the hints that God is giving me about what HE would like me to do with my life, how I fit into his plan to bring as many people as possible to the happiness of knowing him in this life and possessing him in heaven.

As to the answer you get, it will never be mathematically absolute. Even when all the correct signs for a vocation are in place, there will always be some uncertainty until you try it and have it confirmed by someone who speaks for the Church in accepting you and validating your vocation (bishop, religious superior). And they can't accept you until they get to know you and see how you do when you try to follow it.

So once you discern, you have to be ready to take the plunge.

---

high school girl

I believe that I am being called to be a nun. However, I am only 16 and my parents are not very open to the idea (my mother is not a very strong Catholic and my father is an agnostic). Despite their opposition, I want to give my life to Christ. I am not sure where to start. I have no spiritual director and I have not talked to my priest. I was wondering if you had any advice on where to start. I realize that I am very young and I have a while to discern and determine if this is what God wants of me.

Dear Sheila,

You are not too young to feel a vocation. I know many young men and young women who as early as the 7th grade discovered that they had a call.

Of course feeling it is not enough, it has to be tested; not everyone who feels he has a vocation is in fact called.

Start right where you are. You think Christ is calling you to give yourself completely to him. One very strong sign that this might be a true call is the fact that there is no pressure from outside moving you; it seems to be something God is doing in your heart: it has arisen in your soul all by itself. So treat it with care and gratitude.

55

high school boy

What suggestions do you have for a high school freshman who thinks he may be called to the priesthood?

Dear Phil,

Before suggesting anything let me congratulate you – and the promise that even though I don't know you personally, I will remember 'Phil' in my rosary.

It is great that you are open to the priesthood. Don't forget to offer yourself to Christ every time you meet him in confession and Communion. There is a lot for his priests to do in the world today.

Let me start with a question: 'Do you want to move on your vocation right away, and would your parents approve of this?' There are high schools for young men of your age who are thinking of the priesthood. If your parents approve, you should get in touch with one of those schools, visit it, have your parents see it, and see if that is the way Christ wants you to go.

If you think he wants you to cultivate your vocation at home for now, there are several resolutions you need to make right now.

One, grow in your spiritual life (state of grace, sacraments, rosary, make time for God each day). Find a spiritual director who can help you with this and the following points.

Two, do something for others. (Help out occasionally at a soup kitchen, hospital, orphanage. Teach CCD to younger kids. Get some of your friends that might be drifting away back to the Church...)

Three, continue to learn more about your faith (books, tapes, etc.).

Four, start getting to know priests and visiting seminaries until you find where God wants you to go.

Five, stay healthy, play sports, do physical work – wimps are unqualified for the priesthood.

Six, take your present duties to heart – this is one of the best ways to prepare yourself.

I hope you find these points helpful.

Again, I will pray for you, and I hope God gives you the wonderful gift of a vocation. God bless.

---

lost high schooler

I am definitely considering the vocation of priesthood. I am still currently in high school. What should I do? How do I start? I am very lost. Thank you for your time.

Dear Bart,

Maybe you feel lost because you don't know what to do or where to turn with this thought of the priesthood that has come to you – but you have to remember that your feelings are only part of the picture.

You are not lost because you are not on your own. The thoughts that come to you about the priesthood, the desire to become one, came from somewhere else, or rather from Someone else, and not from yourself.

How can that be true if you know you are really thinking them, and you are not hearing voices? Well, Jesus tells us that we can do nothing without him. St Paul said even more specifically that we cannot say the name Jesus without the Holy Spirit – much less think of giving our whole life to Jesus as his priest. So He is the one behind these thoughts.

So now the first thing you have to do is stay close to him, and especially trust him. You are dealing here with God, but God who is very close – so close that you receive him in Communion, and so close that he can speak to your heart (like in your attraction to the priesthood) almost without you realizing it is him.

Make sure you go to Mass often, and receive him as often as you can in Communion. This is where you are going to get the most light as regards figuring out what he wants you to do, and where you will get the strength to do always what is best. And say a prayer every day to Mary for her help. It doesn't have to be a long one, but just every day: three Hail Marys for this intention will make a huge difference. If you pray the rosary offer up one decade with this intention.

Being that you are still in high school, it would be good to bring your parents into the picture. Their advice will be helpful, especially if they are practicing Catholics, and because of your age you will need their OK if you are going to take any practical step to follow your vocation while you are still in high school.

It would be good to talk over with them what your next step should be, to see with them if you should look for a high school where you can finish off the years you still have to do and at the same time prepare yourself for seminary (sometimes these schools are called high school seminaries, or apostolic schools, or some other name), or if you should finish out your high school at home.

The answer to this question will depend to a certain degree on your age and grade, and the type of school you are in.

As you think it through, ask yourself questions like: Will the friends I have now help me follow my vocation? Am I doing as well in school as I should? How am I spending my time?

Another thing to have on the burner is the type of priest you think you should be. What does God seem to be attracting you towards... service as a pastor in a parish? Missionary work? A religious congregation? Contemplative life? The answer to this question (even if it is that you don't know) will be of help to you as you start looking into it more, because God has a concrete path for you, and he will make sure you get enough hints to know what it is.

I hope this gets you started, or at least helps reduce your confusion.

---

one year of college remaining

I am a 21-year-old student at a secular university. Over the past year I have come to hear God's call to the priesthood and I have talked with my diocesan vocations director about entering the seminary. I feel a very strong call to serve God as a priest and I find myself anxious to enter the seminary. However, I am a college junior and I was advised by my vocations director to finish my secular degree. I see the wisdom in this; it is important to be prepared for life if my calling is not true, and I am only a year away from graduation. My question is: With one year left until I graduate, I find that I am yearning for that seminary experience and have trouble concentrating on my studies. How can I keep focused on my secular education, something I do value, and keep my urge for seminary at a healthy level? Thank you.

Dear Nate,

Make the priesthood more and more the center of your life.

Don't think to yourself that you will start studying for the priesthood when you enter the seminary in more than a year's time. Begin now. Take as many credits as you can carry well, even if it's more than you are required.

Why? Because it will enrich your preparation for the priesthood. Don't view your studies as something you are doing just in case you don't have a vocation. They are part of God's path for you to the priesthood.

At the same time, develop and deepen your prayer life: this will keep you from getting discouraged and will give you the spiritual drive and motivation to do as well as you can. And get involved in the parish, teach CCD next year, start or help out in the youth group, etc. That will teach you a lot, and you might even bring someone else into the seminary with you next year. God bless.

DATING AND DISCERNMENT

Once you are looking into a vocation, does your behavior have to change in any way? Is it the same as any other career or a choice of college?

Our society tends to tell us that you have to date in order to be normal and healthy, yet the young person thinking about the vocation senses there is something different in his own case although he may not quite be able to put his finger on it.

It is important to note that when we talk here about dating and relationships, we are talking about more than the normal friendships that young people have as they grow up. You have friends, there is a group of you that like doing things together, maybe you even like some more than others and enjoy their company particularly, but that is as far as it goes. That is what we call friendship. When we speak about dating we are talking about the individual, cultivated friendship, where there is special interest in the other person and it becomes quasi-exclusive.

The questions and answers below, some of them a little on the long side, may help you in your reflections.

---

discernment and relationships

For some time now I've been considering religious life. The more I think about it the more I feel that this is my vocation. Reading about saints such as St Therese for example, only increases that desire to love God, to serve His people and to attain union with Him. However, I have never been in a serious relationship with a member of the opposite sex. Is it possible for me to deepen my love of God, to reach such a level in terms of my spirituality without experiencing that particular type of love on a human level? Can I enter religious life without such an experience?

Dear Brigid,

Your question brings up a topic that causes much confusion because it seems so reasonable.

Many will tell you that you must first experience human love for a member of the opposite sex before being able to give yourself to God. Often it is implied that unless you experience such a love, you will never really mature, you will never know what you are giving up, and you will be therefore more vulnerable in the future – so, better get the experience behind you and then move on.

Remember, we are talking here not about normal friendship (admiration and enjoyment of another person's presence, simply liking a particular individual of the opposite sex) but something more – going further and cultivating a deeper, more personal and usually exclusive relationship through personal dating.

Three things disturb me about this approach:

First, I think it is both masochistic and callous. What you are being asked to do is to play around with your own heart and with someone else's. You are being told that, even though you are pretty sure you might have a vocation, you should seek the love of a person of the opposite sex and do what it takes to make it grow, simply in order to have the experience of love for another on a human level.

But just think a little. If you are normal, the outcome of such an attachment is for your heart to yearn for the union and human fulfillment that love for another naturally makes you desire, and every fiber in you is going to want. In a healthy context, everything in a serious relationship will point toward marriage, and if marriage is not possible, the relationship is ended.

In our Catholic context, the only place for a serious relationship is where there is openness toward marriage and the possibility of marriage (people who are already married don't date others), yet the possibility of marriage is precisely what you have ruled out from the outset, because you believe God is asking something else of you.

That is masochism – useless, self-inflicted, heart-breaking punishment. I fail to see how the frustration this sets you up for can be healthy, either for your soul or for your psychology.

On top of this you are asked to do the same to another person: deliberately lead him on and create in him a thirst that you have no intention of ever satisfying. Such callous disregard for another person's life and emotions—playing with them—can hardly be called love and is hardly the best advertisement or preparation for religious life, since your intention from the outset is to ditch him no matter what.

Some people may discover their vocation after they have been in love, perhaps even deeply, with another person. True. But that is not what we are talking about here, as you can understand. They were open to marriage, but God led them elsewhere. God can lead us by many different paths. But let him do the leading.

The second thing that disturbs me is the underlying, implicit concept here of the type of person that gets a vocation.

It seems to hint that God does not call normal people to a vocation. It seems to imply that if God calls you, you will no longer be subject to the dynamics of your human nature. But you are.

That is why, when someone thinks God is calling him to the priesthood or consecrated life, he realizes right away that his dealings with persons of the opposite sex are going to have to change. He will no longer do things, go places or spend his time in ways that will favor an emotional 'click' with that 'someone special' he knows is out there somewhere. He will be very circumspect in his dealings with others, much like the engaged woman will change the pattern of her dealings with men who are not her fiancé. If they don't, they both know that these relationships have the possibility of destroying the love they have and want to build their lives and futures around.

If you have a vocation, you have to realize that your nature is still the same (yes, of course, you do have the help of grace), so your instinct should be to protect your vocation like she does her future marriage.

The third disturbing thing is that the point of view we are considering does not seem to grasp the essence of a vocation, which is a recklessly generous response—in exclusive love—to Christ who calls. You could almost say that it is essential to a vocation that you could easily do something else good with your life (Christian marriage), but he asks this of you. He asks you to love in a whole new way. You are giving up not something bad but something good to which you have a perfect right. Instead of giving yourself to the pursuit of human love (or more precisely, finding and pleasing God through human love and responsibility), you give yourself directly to him.

This is a very different type of love, and I have found that sometimes the experience of human love can even make it more difficult to love in this spiritual way. The reason is that human love includes a huge proportion of emotional and concrete feedback, that is why it grips us so; the senses have their fill – you can speak, listen to, watch the person you love. Even as the love between spouses grows more spiritual with time, physical presence is an essential component, so much so that marriage vows are taken only 'until death do us part.' Just compare all this to kneeling in front of the Eucharist, which is where we most experience Christ's presence and love, and you will see just how different the two are.

However, this much is true: we do need to experience love in order to follow a vocation.

We cannot follow one without learning to love more deeply, but not necessarily in a 'serious relationship with a member of the opposite sex.' Most of us have experienced love in our families, have seen the goodness and the realities of human love in our parents and other couples close to us. We have seen the joy and the sacrifice, the sublime and the humdrum, and have reaped the fruits of their fidelity. On a spiritual level we have experienced God's love and pardon. We have benefited from those who gave their lives to serve Christ before us: our pastors, the sisters we knew, etc.

There is another point too, and here I will end because this is getting too long: you mentioned the saints you like to read about, especially Saint Therese. The fact of the matter is, many of them gave themselves directly to Christ (Therese was so young she had to get a special dispensation in order to enter the cloister) without going through 'serious relationships' first. If it was good enough for her, why not for you?

God bless.

---

how can I keep my feet on the ground?

Hi! I am a 17-year-old female discerning a religious vocation. Not too abnormal! I know several other people doing so as well. A couple of them feel held back because of a dating relationship. My problem is the opposite! As a senior in high school, I have never dated. And I get pickier and pickier every day! (Has to be Catholic, somewhat intelligent, etc.). Earlier this year I tried to find a boyfriend, but when I tried to do that, I took my eyes off God. My spiritual director told me that I should date at least some before I make any decisions. Any suggestions on how to get a guy but keep a square head on my shoulders while I continue to discern? Thank You!

Dear Becky,

I have to disagree with your spiritual director. As long as you have had normal friendships, and your emotional development is also normal, the dating experience is not absolutely necessary.

You see what happened to your friends who are also discerning: you start dating, then you get to like the guy, then you have the problem: I like him, I would like to marry him – did God send him to me, or was it God telling me before that I had a religious vocation?

The fact of the matter is, we are all human, and if you date, sooner or later you are usually going to find either 'that special person' or one that is 'special enough.' The fact that you are picky means you have your head on your shoulders, and you have seen for yourself that if you become over-involved with someone it takes you away from what is important.

My advice is: Be yourself, enjoy what God has given you, and give priority to your vocation without worrying about everything else.

---

a boy's question too

I am entering high school this year and am deeply considering religious life. While in high school I know there is peer pressure to date. If I am considering a religious vocation to the priesthood, should I date girls in high school? Also, how do you get other teens in the parish to participate more in Life Teen, and in things like eucharistic adoration, Bible study, daily Mass, since they all say they do not have friends in it?

Dear Kenny,

If you are entering high school and are already thinking pretty seriously about a vocation, you may want to speak with your parents about going to a high school that focuses on the priesthood, such as a high school seminary. These are for boys in just your position, but they are not for everyone, so you would have to visit, see how it is, get advice from the directors of the school, and see what your parents think.

If this is not an option, then you have to give priority to your vocation. Take part in all the usual activities at school, but take care of your vocation. Go to Mass as often as you can and build up your prayer life. I am glad to see you want to get your friends involved in good activities too. You are not going to get everyone the first time, but keep trying. Make sure you organize fun but constructive things you can all do together.

I want a boyfriend

Hello, I'm 14 and very into my religion (Catholic of course), I LOVE being Catholic – it is the most exciting thing EVER to be in CHRIST'S Church!!!!

But now I will narrow it down to my question. I have a problem, since I'm ONLY 14 I guess it is typical that I would want a boyfriend. And lately, I really do want one, I have never really had one, and would like to see what it is like. And since I am a typical teen, I have crushes. If I do ever get one, I assure you he will be Catholic. At times, I think about having a boyfriend, just to be crazy around, and to be myself, and most of all, to talk about the faith with and so on.

My question is: Is it wrong for me to want a boyfriend at the same time I'm considering being a religious? I know I can't have both, but I don't know what God is calling me to. Would it be wrong for me, if I ever got one? And one more thing, I have thoughts of having a boyfriend, not for sexual reasons, or anything IMPURE, but just to be myself around. Is it wrong for me to have these thoughts?

Dear Joy,

What a refreshing, bubbly letter! Let's get to the core of it. You are 14, you think at times you might be called to consecrate your life to God, but (because you are 14) you would love to have a boyfriend as well, and you want to know if that would be wrong.

I don't know if you did so on purpose or not, but you hit on something that is fundamental in a vocation and will have very concrete consequences when you become a nun, and it's this: to give yourself to God, to really love him in the exclusive way a priest or religious does, you give up not only what is bad, but also many things that are good.

Marriage is good. Attachment to our family is good. Possessions and success in life are good, but when we consecrate ourselves to Christ we put all those and many other good things to one side. So, in order to answer your question about getting a boyfriend, especially if your intentions are not bad, we have to broaden our reflections.

Before we begin, a general point or two about having a boyfriend. It is funny how we talk about getting a boyfriend or getting a girlfriend almost as if we were talking about a thing, something I am going to pick up, enjoy or use, and perhaps throw away when I'm done.

But a boyfriend is another person, with personal worth, with all the attraction that God put in boys for girls, and even though you might pick him as you pick a blouse (yes, this one is nice, it suits me), things don't usually stop there. You have met a person, and a whole dynamic begins. His different way of thinking, his different sensitivity and reactions, everything tends to draw and create interest, bonds, attachment in you.

And he finds the same or greater fascination in you.

Then you begin to depend on each other, and the attachment grows – or if you split up for some reason you have more expectations and hopes in the next boyfriend.

What I am getting at is that having a boyfriend is not a casual thing, something we can pick up and then shrug off lightly. Having an individual boyfriend with whom you are going to open your soul and spirit is a major step and should not be rushed into. It may be a bit soon at 14.

Having a group of friends, some of whom are boys, and finding that there are some boys that you like being around more than the others is fine, good and natural. Participating in youth groups, having your crushes, doing school things, enjoying mixed company are all part of normal growing up and not bad in themselves. So now let's get back to your question.

You are pretty sure you might be called to be a religious. What does this mean? That God may be calling you to be his spouse, to love him totally, to make him your everything, to set aside any other love and choose only him.

What you have to do now is keep that in the forefront. You will meet boys, have crushes on boys, feel the natural desire to have children, and all this will attract you because you are normal. But through all this there will be something more in your mind and soul. Since you know that God may be offering you the treasure of his love, and may have chosen you for himself, you will make sure that you always keep him in first place.

You will make sure you don't put yourself in a situation where other loves or attachments may grow and get in the way of God's love.

Does that help?

---

human nature!

Veronica opens her heart and writes the sincerest reflection on human nature and the struggles of a love that wants to be generous with God. It is good and helpful reading, but just look at those opening lines, and then see at the end her wonderful openness and generosity.

Hi! I'm a 19-year-old college sophomore. A very good friend and I started dating (chastely!) several months ago with his stipulation that he doesn't distract me in my vocation discernment. Um...it's a little late for that!

Perhaps his holiness in action or fervor in prayer initially drew me to him, but I knew a few weeks after meeting him that he is 'the one' – IF God is calling me to the vocation of holy matrimony. (I can't explain how, but I felt a peace about it.) However, more and more I notice the quiet insistence inside that I check into consecrated life.

Through my parents' example I've observed some of the joys, rewards, sufferings, sacrifices, etc. of marriage. At this point all I can see of religious life consists of the joys and rewards (e.g. simplicity, poverty, structured prayer time, daily Mass & Eucharistic Adoration, a strong community of fellow believers, freedom (without a biological family dependent on me) to reach out to those suffering and in need).

With that said, I acknowledge that I need to explore this type of life to better observe all its facets (and hopefully visit a few convents in the near future). Trying to figure out my future calling has caused me much anxiety and robbed me (at times) of the gift of joy God has given to me. Praise Him for helping me finally recognize a few things! Worrying about my vocation: (1) indicates that I'm not trusting in Christ (who knows what he's doing) but rather in myself (who haven't a clue); (2) means that I have taken my focus off Peace himself, or I wouldn't be in a perpetual state of unrest; (3) steals away the moment that is now, in which I should selflessly live for the Lord and strive to glorify him, rather than live for myself, constantly dwelling on ME, what I should do, MY feelings and contributions, etc.

Thankfully, God is very patient with me and helps me daily as I strive to take myself from my own clumsy hands and give myself entirely over to his care (slowly but surely!).

Another thing: sometimes I have an inner peace about the aforementioned relationship, so why do I become so unsettled at other times? Christ granted me the deepest peace I have ever felt the two times I surrendered completely to his will—whatever vocation it meant—for my future (through many, many tears and pleas for help).

My mom tells me to let the discovery of my vocation sit on the back burner for now (at least while I'm at school) unless God makes it clear for me to do otherwise. She says I can be happy in anything I choose to do, but another great friend of mine and my boyfriend's (coincidentally a future nun) tells me that a vocation is a fulfillment of who a person is, and we will be our happiest only in the vocation to which God has called us.

What should I do? Should I stop spending extra time with my boyfriend, or not worry about this for now? By the way, I've discussed this all with him several times and he encourages me to give this all to God and follow His will, regardless of how it might affect him. (He has even referred to himself as a possible 'stepping stone' in my life-path.) It really, really hurts me to think of severing (or even restricting) our friendship and/or relationship, but if he innocently impedes my ability to give my all to Jesus, I need to gently separate from him unless/until God leads me back to him. (Am I correct in my thinking?) What do you suggest I do?

Dear Veronica,

Your first few lines say it all. They are a lesson in human nature, a lesson we don't learn too readily. But then the rest of your message shows how, despite ourselves, God's graces have such a respectful but insistent power to make themselves present in our lives, and how generous you really want to be with God.

You started dating 'on one condition,' and now 'it is too late (for it not to affect your vocation discernment).' I would say you forgot for a while what we are made of, and now you have found out again. Except that now your knowledge of human nature is no longer theory, it is happening to you: God made man for woman, and woman for man. Everything in each complements the other: physically, emotionally, psychologically, spiritually. And if you are striving to live a good Christian life, and he is too, the points of attraction are going to be more, not less! So you find your attachment growing.

St Teresa of Avila, who was no cynic, only an intelligent, practical, down-to-earth saint with a piercing understanding of human nature and a sense of humor to go with it, used to say in Spanish: 'entre santa y santo, pared de cal y canto' – a rhyming phrase that means: 'if you have a holy man and a holy woman, you'd better build a stone wall between them.' That explains what has happened to you. Now, despite this experience there still is an insistent voice that comes back. This should make you think.

What about your conflicting feelings? Dreams of marriage—especially in the context of doing what God wants and with a person who is obviously one in a million—have naturally got to bring peace because it directly satisfies your spiritual as well as emotional needs and the instinct for motherhood God has placed in you as a woman. It is perfect. You would have to be strange to feel otherwise.

But then that voice that seems to ruin it all, saying, 'Go check out consecrated life.'

The anxiety you feel may be in part the normal struggle felt by anyone called by God to give up the goods of this life that they can see and touch, and instead choose him, whom we can neither see nor touch nor have a direct give-and-take with.

We can only win this struggle by faith, faith that is belief and trust, faith that you nourish in the Eucharist.

You are experiencing the beginning of human love. Now, ask Jesus to touch your heart with divine love, to enter into that whole new dimension of love for him, like him. He did not grasp onto his divinity, hold onto what he had as Son of God; instead, he humbled himself, gave up what it was to be Son of God, and became one like us in everything but sin, in order to save us. He really emptied himself; for him it was such a step down – much more than he asks of us. And when he was here as a man, he chose to love us and love his Father with his whole human heart. You need to ask him to take your heart and make it like his.

What should you do now? Should you stop spending extra time with your boyfriend? I think you know the answer; you practically said it. If you spend time with him, most probably your attachment is going to grow. Ask yourself if that is what you want, if it is going to make it easier or more difficult to find out if God wants you all for himself, and if it is going to make it easier or not for you to follow him if he does. That is really what is in the balance.

It won't be the easiest, but now it's your turn to show Christ you love him like the martyrs, and that you trust in him as they did. God bless. I am sure his grace will continue to strengthen and lead you.

---

sin to date?

I'm almost 15 and almost positive I want to become a nun and missionary. I know this means taking the vow of chastity and accepting Christ as my spouse. With this in mind, would it be a sin to date in high school?

Dear Serena,

I think you are asking the wrong question, or maybe the right one the wrong way. The question 'is such-and-such a sin?' is a basic one, and when we are making decisions it is very important. The first thing we need to do if we want to please Christ and be his follower is avoid sin. OK. But that is not everything.

It is never enough just to avoid sin. Our Christian life is about growth, and growth in love. Just imagine how strange it would seem if your Dad were to ask you, 'Do you think it would be a sin if I didn't buy Mom some roses for our anniversary?' He would definitely be asking the wrong question, don't you think?

So, you are pretty sure God is giving you a vocation. You seem to be willing to give him everything. The question then is not: Will it be a sin to date? – but: Will dating be the best way to show God I will put him in the first place, and will it help me keep him there?

But just so there won't be any mistakes here, you have to be clear as to what you mean by dating. I have found some kids refer to normal friendships, and when groups of friends do things together, as 'dating,' but what we mean here is the pursuit of a pretty exclusive friendship between a boy and a girl.

Now, in the culture in which we live, granted our inherent personal weakness and the pressures around us, that may not be the thing to do too soon, even if you don't have a vocation.

The pressure is always there, and they are going to try to make you feel you are strange if you don't do what everyone else is into, but don't get drawn into it. Get a good group of friends, whose parents are like your own, and you can have lots of healthy fun and activity without getting drawn away from God. And keep close to Christ in prayer (rosary, Mass).

---

distractions

These feelings and confusions are not limited to the women. Men have them too. Like Alex:

I think the Lord is calling me to be celibate. I've been more or less leading a celibate life this year. However, lately there have been some distractions. There are a couple girls who are infatuated with me. I am scheduled to eat out with one of them next week. I really like them, and these distractions are not only distracting but confusing. They make me wonder: Am I really called to celibacy? Is it OK or good or pleasing to the Lord to become friends with these two girls even if I think he is calling me to be celibate?

Dear Alex,

From the other answers in this forum you see that our feelings and attractions remain even if we are called to celibacy. Let me give you some further tips.

One, you have to know yourself. For example, if you are the type of person who gets involved with people—takes a personal interest in them, feels for them, etc.—you know you will find it difficult to maintain a certain independence in a friendship. It is good to know this about yourself.

Two, you have to be practical. Certain things, like friendship and attachment between the sexes, come unbidden. They can hamper the recognition of God's call.

Three, the hint that you feel that God might be asking celibacy of you seems to be pretty strong. It is a hunch worth following up on. If you go out with a girl, I suggest that you also find time to be alone with Christ. Drop into a church and talk with him a while. Go on a good spiritual retreat that will challenge you.

Four, the importance of point three is: if you get interested in a certain girl more than others, you will find yourself declining invitations so as to be more with her. If Christ may be calling you to be celibate, you will find yourself having to decline other invitations because of where your heart is. That is the core of celibacy. God bless.

OTHER PROBLEMS AND DOUBTS IN DISCERNMENT

---

not sure

I am a 16-year-old girl who is interested in becoming a nun. Nothing I could think of would make me happier. The problem is I do not feel that I am quite worthy of this sacred vocation. What would be the first step in determining whether or not this is indeed the Lord's will for me? Thanks.

Dear Gabrielle,

No one is worthy of a vocation. Just like no one is worthy of being a Christian. It is a grace that God gives.

If you are thinking of it, there is already the chance that you are being called. If you want to love God above all things, that would be further evidence. If you know what you give up, and are convinced that what you have to give up is good and beautiful too (your own preferences, marriage and a family, certain possessions) but you want to do it out of love for God, that might make it even clearer.

I don't think you can go any further in knowing God's will without actually doing something to try to find out where. You are probably already thinking of some group in particular, so make contact with them and see what happens.

---

it keeps coming back

I recently attended a retreat for vocations and after that retreat, I came to the conclusion that religious life was not for me. I was at peace with the idea that I was being called to married life. I went to a prayer session and during that prayer the idea came back; I even went to sleep and dreamt about being a Franciscan.

I honestly thought that I was at peace with the idea. I am not sure why I am thinking about it again. I am currently seeing somebody, he is very spiritual. I can honestly say that he has brought me closer to God. I don't understand. If God wants me to become his bride, why would he send this guy into my life? I used to be more materialistic, and since he's been into my life I don't even care about these things anymore.

My boyfriend has really shown me that nothing in this life matters but my soul. He believes that once I take care of my soul everything else would fall into place. I thought that God sent him into my life so we can have a family later on... but then again at times I feel like the Lord is calling me to be his bride. Many people have approached me and ask me if I am thinking about being a nun; a priest even asked me that. Please help.

Dear Tammy,

Not a doubt that God is hard to figure out at times. Let's take it by parts.

If you have a vocation, it does not mean there is no man out there that you could love and who would be very good for you, even spiritually speaking. I guess if we were the ones who were giving out vocations we would tend to say, 'This is what I want you to do and it is your only shot at holiness, so you'd better take it.' God is not like that.

Our vocation is what he wants us to do, where we fit in, in his best-case scenario. He makes the invitation, he sends us the messengers, he makes sure we have the opportunity to hear the call – but he never forces us. It even seems that most times there is ample room for doubt as regards our vocation, precisely because he never forces it on us. He attracts us. He gives us the chance to show our love in trust and generosity. And there is no big stick.

Let me rephrase your question. You thought you had solved the vocation question, but it has come back. The striking aspect to what you say is that these thoughts are definitely not something you have sought, and they have increased as you have become more spiritually minded. What confuses you is this, that the person who seems to be the 'culprit' for your spiritual growth and renewal (and hence in great part for your thinking about the vocation) is precisely someone who seems sent by God as a top-drawer find for a good marriage.

Maybe this will help. Keep your feet on the ground, from the point of view of faith. Look at reality. Your boyfriend has encouraged you to grow spiritually and straighten out your priorities. He has been God's instrument in that. Now it seems God is building on this gift he gave you in him. Your thoughts and the impression others seem to have is also reality.

I think you owe it to yourself, to God, and to your boyfriend to look into your vocation. Don't try to figure out why God did things this way, just live reality. Give God his place. Give the souls that may need you their place. Give him a chance to make his will more clear to you by actively testing your vocation.

And what about your boyfriend? Who knows what plans God may have for him, and what part your example is going to have in him discovering what God wants of him. But of this much be sure: if you have a vocation, he is not the last 'perfect' man you are going to meet in your life. And each time you do, you are going to choose God above any creature of his.

---

hoping I don't have a vocation

The thought has come to me in prayer, very grudgingly, that I might have a vocation. But I am petrified and I don't want one. Sometimes I feel like the only way to serve Christ is through a vocation, but I desire a husband and many children very much. It would be a huge sacrifice to give that up. I often avoid the thought as much as possible. I am going to try and visit a convent this summer to give God first chance, but I am going with the hope that I will find I don't have a vocation to the religious life. Am I just running away from it, or does feeling like a vocation would be such a sacrifice mean that I don't have one?

Dear Jenny,

The fear and almost horror that grips you when you think you might have a vocation cannot of itself tell you if you have a vocation or not. It could be due to the fact that you instinctively, spiritually understand you don't have one, and then again it may be due to your attachment to something of itself more attractive and satisfying on the surface than a vocation – something good in itself and that has been a major part of your dreams and plans up to the present – and now the vocation is intruding on it all.

So how do you sort it out, how do you figure out if it is one extreme or the other or something in between?

You have to pray. You have to ask yourself some questions. You have to let it sink in that if God is calling you the way to respond is in love and generosity, and not 'kicking and screaming.'

When you pray, don't center on 'God, tell me what you want me to do.' Prayer is much more than that. Thank him for all he has done for you. Try to absorb yourself into the mystery of God, how Christ is human as well as divine, how it was not easy for his human nature to give up his life for us yet he did so, for example. Adore God in your prayer, give him his place as your Creator. Intercede for others in your prayer; try to open your mind and heart to their needs and ask God how you can best help them. Of course you should also do what comes more easily in prayer – ask for what you need. Tell God to help you if it is generosity you need.

Ask yourself some questions. About life, its purpose, its length. About eternal life. Why has God been so generous with you, etc...

And when the 'panic attacks' surface, step back. Don't let yourself get drawn into them. They are often a sign something is wrong, that you are looking at the wrong things, or looking at them in the wrong way. God bless.

on the way back

I have a dilemma. I have told my immediate family that I am returning to the Catholic Church. I have not shared with them that I think I may have a vocation. They are not practicing Catholics, but all made the same comment when I told them. They said, 'What? Are you gonna be a priest now?' When they said this they did it in a joking manner. This has made me feel very uncomfortable. How should I have handled it? At the time I just changed the subject. I do not want to talk about a possible vocation with them until I am sure.

Dear Rich,

I am not going to tell you how you should have handled it, because it is pointless now—what happened, happened—and, besides, I don't know!

So, instead, let me tell you that right now I think you should concentrate on getting back into the knowledge of and close personal relationship with Christ in the Eucharist, which is the center of our faith. Establish a prayer life, get back to the Mass and the sacrament of reconciliation, get back into the Gospels, explore the Catechism of the Catholic Church, and bring Mary into your life.

As you do this, Christ will be able to speak to your soul. You will learn to listen to him, and you will gradually find your way to an answer as regards your vocation.

The best time and way to tell your family about it is not, in my opinion, a crucial question at this point, and may perhaps be a little premature. Congratulations on your return! Welcome home.

dryness

Why do I have this dry feeling? (When I was younger I loved to pray.) Why does it feel that everyone is telling me to join the religious life when I am having these dry feelings? (I don't feel that I am worthy to join the religious order at times, but I find peace when I am there.) Please give me some idea of what I am to do since I love the Holy Blessed Trinity and I would love to do what my vocational call is whether it is to be a wife and mother or a nun. I just want to know what I am to do. I don't want to be confused or have this dryness for the rest of my life... Sorry if I sound confusing but I am so very confused.

Dear Nadine,

Let's see what we can make of your confusion. Your main burden now seems to be your dryness, and that is what is coloring and affecting your thoughts about everything else. You feel unworthy of a vocation because of it, and yet you want to love God above all else.

Dryness is good, believe it or not. It gives us the opportunity to see our faith in action, to see if I can go ahead based on what I know rather than how I feel. Dryness doesn't change God or reality outside us; it is only a change inside us. Sometimes dryness is only on the level of our feelings, and sometimes it is much deeper, a real darkness of the soul and test of our faith.

In dryness you have to hold onto and deepen in what you already know for sure: God is there, he loved you so much that he created you, and then sent his Son so you would be free from sin. He is really present in the Eucharist, he takes away your sins in confession, he listens when you pray, he wants what is best for you, he gave you the gift of baptism, and therefore he wants you to bring him to others.

As regards having a vocation or not, there are too many unknowns for me to answer you. Your age, freedom, obligations, and past will all affect the answer.

But let me just tell you something in general: it may be best to pay more attention to praying with your whole heart at this stage. Pick the time you are going to dedicate to prayer each day (Mass, Communion, rosary, some Gospel reading...)—not too much— things that you can do every day without fail, and make them your big act of faith, the special thing you do for God each day to pay back his love, no matter how you feel as you do them. It is for him, not for you, remember.

It seems to me that as soon as you take your mind off your dryness you will see the answer to your vocation question. Your friends seem to! And something very important and favorable: you seem to be open to it and ready to do whatever God wants. This should work out well.

---

rash promise

Hello! I am a young adult female and I have been wondering for some time what the good Lord wants of me... years ago my mother was seriously ill.... I sat and prayed that everything would be okay with her results, and made a promise to God that if this was the case, I would become a nun. Well, at that particular time, I was almost certain I was being called to that way of life. Now, some time later, I still haven't joined the convent and am even wondering if the Lord really wants me to be a nun or possibly get married some day. It seems like a seesaw situation for me. Some days I feel like joining the convent, while other days I feel like being a wife. I don't want to break my promise to the Lord and sin against him. Please help me in my situation!

Dear Nina,

The greatest thing we can do for God is not going away to be a nun, but doing his will.

I am sure that when you made your promise to God it pleased him, because at the time you were nearly certain that that was his will. But if he, after you made the promise, shows you that he wants something else of you, then do what he says. Don't worry, it is never a sin to do what God wants even if you promised him something else.

Now, there is still something very important for you to work out. From what you say above, it is your feelings that are swinging back and forth. It would be unusual if this did not happen: our feelings are like that, fickle as the wind. So, if you base a decision or commitment on feelings, you are going to be very confused in the future, because no matter which you choose (marriage or religious life) it will only take a few days for your feelings to swing back again to the other side.

You have to seek in your soul, in the way God has been leading you, in the principles of faith, in the things that matter most to you, in the advice of someone you trust, what God really wants of you, knowing that no matter what it is, your feelings are going to be sometimes for it and sometimes against.

Then, knowing that, go ahead and opt for what he wants.

---

is it God or me talking?

I am 15 and I think I might want to be a priest and later on become the Pope. Is this a message from the Lord or is it only in my brain?

Dear Mike,

There may be many people who would like to become pope, but I don't think any of them ever will! There are others who want to be bishops and never will either. So that part of the message might be only your imagination or just another of the idealistic, wonderful desires that capture our imagination when life is still all ahead of us. I wouldn't give it any special importance one way or the other, since either way it is not something that depends on what you want.

Where does that leave your desire to be a priest? It may or may not be the beginning of a sign of a vocation. I think it might help you to really think about what it is to be a priest. Read the lives of some saints (St John Vianney, St Maximilian Kolbe, St John Bosco, for example) and discover in them what it is to be a priest, the type of love for God it entails, and the willingness to serve others and suffer for them that it requires.

If what you read sets your heart on fire and makes you want the vocation more, you just may have one.

I'm miserable

Hello! I'm writing from a highly technical university, and ... I'm not very happy at all with my life. The work where I am is hard, yet it's doable. The thing is, I'm not enjoying any of it. I'm at a loss for what I'm supposed to do with my life. I recently became a Eucharistic minister, and I love every second of it. I have had some of the best feelings in my life while I'm serving. I chose to go to the place I'm in now simply because it was the best place I got accepted to. If not for prayer groups and God, I would probably go insane. I see graduates from this place, and they are nothing at all how I would like to be. Although I shouldn't judge others, as Christ is in everyone, I will do anything God wants me to do. Save for my religious activities, I am utterly miserable at this place. What should I do? I want to be happy and serve God at the same time.

Dear Joe,

I think you are focusing too much on your feelings, and when we do that, it means that we are still at the center of our thoughts and decisions. It is OK for our feelings to prod us, but they cannot be the defining element in our decisions. I hope that's clear.

What I mean is, your feelings of frustration and boredom at your present place might trigger reflection as to what value there is to what you are doing; they might get you thinking what life is really about. Once you start on your reflection, you have to set your feelings aside, you have to get to more solid ground, to truths you can build your life on.

Why? Because no matter what vocation in life you follow, you are going to go through a stage—or many stages—of adverse feelings (when things seem to go wrong, when you feel wretched about some aspect of it and feel like giving up).

So when you make a choice in life, you should choose something that brings you happiness and makes you enthusiastic, but not only because it does. The happiness and enthusiasm it brings should stem from something more profound that will still give you direction and stability when the feelings are gone. I would even say you have to choose something that will bring you happiness even when the feeling of happiness is gone.

For example, if because of what you describe above you decide to give your life to Christ as a priest, you will naturally be enthusiastic at the beginning because you have those wonderful feelings when you are close to the Eucharist. But as you go on you will meet people who will reject and may even hate you because of what you preach (Jesus' message is a difficult one: honesty, purity, sacrifice...), and you will have down days. If you choose to follow him now because of the nice feelings, you might abandon him when those feelings are gone.

So I would say: Is God speaking to you through your feelings, telling you something about life and about why he made you? Try to answer that question – why he made you, I mean.

Go to him in the Eucharist and ask him why he gave you life, how you can use it best. Speak about this with a prudent person you trust. Then base your decisions on the truths you discover, and not on the feelings that set the whole process in motion.

---

pressure

I've never really felt a calling to much of anything. But for a long time, I've felt a strong desire to get married and have children. I've been blessed with many talents and also a profound interest in several fields of science. My dilemma comes in that many people at our church feel that I should be a priest. I think this may have something to do with our lack of priests in our diocese and also because I'm one of few youths that frequently helps out and attends events. Not that I'm completely closed to the idea, but I feel like it's being shoved down my throat. Any suggestions as how to deal with this?

Dear Larry,

When something requiring commitment is mentioned to us with some expectation as regards our answer, it is almost automatic to feel that it is being forced on us, especially if we were not thinking of it. You have to deal with this reaction and go beyond it.

Take a look at yourself. You are one of the few youths that frequently help out and attend events. As if that weren't enough, now people seem to think you might be called to be a priest. Almost makes you wish that you were just like everyone else and never showed up in the first place, doesn't it? To crown your confusion and bad luck, you are not closed to the idea, and so think there might be some truth to it, while at the same time you have abilities and are attracted to other ways of life and interests.

One good thing at least is surfacing: you can think, and you are honest with yourself. Maybe that's two. To bring some light into the matter, let's get back to what a vocation is.

A vocation is a call from God. People don't give you a vocation, you can't give yourself one – only God can call you. And even when a spiritual director knows you and encourages you to follow a vocation, all he really is saying that he sees all the signs that God may be calling you.

Now for the other equally important part: only you can answer him, only you can live your vocation. Nobody else can do it for you. Nobody else can give the fruit God is expecting from you.

The question you need to take to God in prayer (your thanksgiving after Communion is a great time to do it, or in a visit to our Lord in the Eucharist) is this: 'You have taken care of me, you gave me a different way of reacting than my friends, you have drawn me to you by helping out and attending events. You have also placed normal desires for marriage and family in my heart. You have made me aware of the needs of those around me, so I am not closed to the priesthood. Do you want to use me as your priest? Is that where you are leading me? Is it you speaking through those people who mention it to me?'

Also spend some time considering two more realities: what Christ has done for you, and the needs people around you have. Then I think you need to offer yourself to God and tell him you are willing to do anything for him.

If as well as the above, you seek out a spiritual director for yourself, you will surely get the answer to your question.

CHAPTER FOUR

Celibacy and Chastity

INTRODUCTION

Celibacy may well be the least-understood area when priest-hood and consecrated life are viewed from the outside. It is seen as an undue imposition. People can't imagine you taking it on freely. People don't readily understand that celibacy is something you are called to and readily live because of the one who calls and the total-ity of the service you want to give.

Celibacy puts the vocation question into perspective: You respond to a call, but you do not dictate the conditions.

---

why?

What are the advantages of celibacy for a Catholic priest?

Dear Juan,

The main value in celibacy is that it is the way of life that Christ chose for himself and his Mother. It makes us more like him.

By celibacy we dedicate ourselves totally and exclusively to loving Christ and his Church, we dedicate ourselves exclusively and totally to serving souls without any hindrance or encumbrance.

Celibacy makes us 'put my money where my mouth is,' as the saying goes. We spend all our time preaching the Kingdom; we tell all who will listen that heaven is greater than all the earth can offer, that Christ deserves everything, that he means more than anything else. Our celibacy means and shows that we really believe what we preach.

Another fruit of our celibacy is the help and inspiration it can give to Catholic parents who are doing their best to be faithful to what Christ asks of them, to be open to life, to be selfless in the way they give themselves to each other. For many, the priest's fidelity is what gives them courage.

---

is this only for Supermen?

I have been thinking about the priesthood for a while now, ever since the sixth grade. Lately, the way things are going has been a bit confusing, and I think my vocation is getting a bit dimmer as the confusion gets worse. My problem is this: I want to be a priest and everything in my life has lead me to the point where the priesthood is the place for me, yet I am easily attracted and stay attracted to girls. I was wondering if this was common or something which could be hinting to me NOT being called to the priesthood? Any help, advice and the like would be most appreciated.

Dear John,

I see nothing more normal than an attraction to girls in a young man. Even though God gave us this for a very good reason and it is part of his plan, it is nevertheless a drive that has to be mastered, whether you are called to the priesthood or the married life. What I mean is this: it is part of God's original plan, but we have a fallen nature and it is not easy to follow God's will in this regards. We have to master our imagination, instincts, desires so as to be faithful to what God wants. The way to master your heart and the drive to love in our life, is to choose whom you are going to love and put all our energies into loving that person.

This might sound strange, to choose whom you are going to love. Yes, attraction happens, but we decide to love. Love costs. A man who marries tells his bride he will love her for richer or poorer, for better or worse. In essence he says, even though someone more attractive might cross my path I am only for you; even though everything does not work out like a dream I will be faithful to you; count on me.

The secret to the heart of a priest, and the reason he can choose celibacy is because he chooses to love Christ, love the Church and love souls in a very particular way, with absolute dedication. And because he has made this love-choice, even if someone attractive comes along, even if things do not work out like a dream, he too is faithful. He knows what he has done, and he reaffirms the choice to love Christ when difficulties arise, and even when they don't.

So I think your attraction is normal. What remains now if you are called to the priesthood is to set your heart to love Christ and center your mind to know him and do his work. Increase your love in prayer. Strengthen your spirit so you can be master of your choices and actions. Don't expect attractions to go away, but pay more attention to what you have chosen.

---

but the Bible says...

Mark, in his question below, calls the whole matter into question, saying that according to Scripture, the requirement of priestly celibacy is an aberration.

Just the other day I was reading the Bible (the non-copyrighted version) and I found something that seems very wrong regarding the Catholic views on vocations. My problem is: If someone wants to become a priest, for example, the Catholic view is that you cannot ever become married or enter into a relationship with another person. When I was reading the Bible the other day, it said that running a family is a requirement for being a priest. So where do your ideas come from? Thank you.

Dear Mark,

Fortunately, they are not my ideas, meaning that I did not come up with them. But you probably mean by 'your ideas' those of the Catholic Church.

Like most of the ideas of the Catholic Church, this one has its roots in Scripture and in the example of Christ; it then matured and developed under the action of the Holy Spirit in the living Tradition of the Catholic Church.

It is a fact that many of the first priests—presbyters—of the Church may have been married, and some of them definitely were. You are probably referring to Titus 1: 5-6, in which Paul says that he left Titus in Crete to appoint 'presbyters in every town... on condition that a man be blameless, married only once, with believing children' who basically were not a cause of scandal.

Now, if you had to be married in order to be a priest, then Paul himself could not have become one. We know he was not married because, when he gave advice to the Corinthians about marriage, he said that he wished all could be like himself, free of marriage to dedicate themselves wholly to the Lord, but if they did marry it would not be a wrong thing to do. So running a family is not a requirement for becoming a priest. All Paul says is that for a married man to be ordained he cannot have been married more than once and must have brought up his family well.

You have, however, opened an interesting question. Is it not a big jump to go from where Paul is to where the Catholic Church (Latin Rite) now stands, saying that only unmarried men can be ordained, and that they may not marry afterwards? What justifies such a jump?

A priest is another Christ, and he works 'in the person of Christ.' Christ's example is paramount for a priest, and is the pattern for his life. Christ did not marry. Christ spoke about giving up father, mother, wife... for the Kingdom. He said that some are incapable of marriage relationships either by nature or by mutilation, but others have voluntarily given up marriage for the sake of the Kingdom. The apostle John was not married. As we saw, Paul was not married either.

From the very beginning of Christianity, there were many who gave themselves voluntarily to God as virgins and lived their call faithfully. What the Church realized was that celibacy went so well with the priesthood (it was what Christ chose for himself, it shows you really believe in heaven, it leaves you free to give yourself totally to your people, among other reasons) that it decided in the Latin Church that God did not give the charism of the priesthood without granting the charism of celibacy as well. So nowadays if you cannot live celibacy it means you are not being called to the priesthood.

Sound impossible? Christ told Peter it was impossible for men, but possible with God's help. God bless.

---

couldn't I have both?

I am currently a senior in high school and I have felt called by God from events as early as second grade. I am certain of the fact that God has called me to religious life. Now I have the real pressing question... Where? I have a girlfriend for whom I deeply care and am considering married deacon-hood, but would this be enough? I was also considering becoming a Episcopalian priest and then later converting to Catholicism with a wife, but would this be truthful, considering that I would never willingly break myself truly free from the Catholic Church? What about the Byzantines? (I don't understand how it's an 'American' tradition for those Catholics to not marry, since most American religious men are Protestants that allow marriage of the ordained.) Complete priesthood involves rejecting so many amoral things in life that it hardly seems like a natural response to God at times. Didn't he instruct the first man and woman to 'be fertile and multiply' (Gen 1:28)? I understand that the first priests and bishops denied themselves of this to better devote their time to the Church, but what about Paul's words in 1 Cor 7:2,9)? Wouldn't a wife keep a priest out of trouble and satisfy a basic human need? Also... didn't the first apostles make a conscientious decision to not marry without a written law telling them not to? I understand you lack the authority to change the traditions of the Catholic Church, but what can I do to better understand the reasoning behind this?

Dear Kevin,

Your question is quite exhaustive and touches on a point that is central to understanding the nature of the priesthood. The promise of remaining celibate that a priest makes is not inherent to the priesthood, but it is the way of life that the Church in its experience over the centuries has discovered is the most fitting human response to the mystery of the priesthood.

Basically what you ask, and answer, is: is there any way round the promise of celibacy? Could you possibly become a priest and be married at the same time? Then you ask if God is not contradicting himself when he tells our first parents to increase and multiply, yet tells his priests not to. Or would it be OK to opt for married diaconate instead of the priesthood?

Remember where you are coming from, Kevin. You already have a girlfriend and you care for her very much. So celibacy is not an abstraction for you: it would mean giving up a special person you already know, and a way of life that is good and attractive and a distinct possibility for you. Nevertheless, the impression that God may be calling you to a priest has been there for some time, to the degree that you are pretty sure that you have a vocation.

You are right to want to know the reasons for celibacy. There is much at stake.

Remember the story Jesus told about the man who collected pearls? He had a fine collection but one day saw a remarkable pearl that was so beautiful and valuable that it was worth the sum of all he had already collected. He immediately went out and sold all his magnificent collection so as to be able to buy that one special pearl. It would have been dumb to do so if the pearl weren't so great. It's the same with the priesthood. Unless you really know the value of it, you will not see why you should give up all the other things that look so good to you.

Now, only our faith can help us understand what the priest-hood is, and its real value. Only faith can tell us how much Jesus loved us, and give us the desire to love him back as much. Only faith can give us trust, and enable us to start out on a journey that seems too long and too harsh if we don't know who is going to help us along the way.

What do I mean by faith? An abstract idea? No, it is knowing what Christ did for us, and what he continues to do for us. It is know-ing that in the Mass you renew the sacrifice he offered on the Cross so that all those present can share in its graces; it is knowing that he is present in the Eucharist for us, to be with us. It is to know that Christ takes away our sins in Reconciliation. To know that he does all this through the hands of his priest. Love is to give yourself to oth-ers, to be always at their service; to want to be available to help, heal them from their sins, give them encouragement and hope, bear their burdens; love is to spend your life not centered on yourself but on someone else. Celibacy makes us able to do this in the extreme.

When you become a priest, Christ takes hold of you in a special way. He has you do his work, but that is never enough. Priesthood is not a career or a job – he draws you ever more to be like him. The priest needs to become identified with Christ, to think, feel and live like he did. To have his same standards and motivations. To become like him. And Jesus never married. By choice. So the best way for a priest is Christ's way. By choice.

God wants us to 'increase and multiply,' but for a priest it is going to be in a spiritual way. A priest is called to give life to souls, to care for them, educate them, protect them, challenge them, at times correct them, give them example, give his life for them. Just as Jesus did. When St Paul described his relationship with the Christians in the cities where he preached the Gospel he called them his 'children' that he 'brought into life.' That is why we call our priests 'Father.'

Also, one of the major truths that our faith teaches us and we should base our lives and choices on is that there is an afterlife, that the soul is worth more than the body because it lasts forever. Celibacy in a priest shows he really believes that and has staked his life on it.

I have only skimmed the surface here, Kevin. You will find more in the encyclical letter written by Pope Paul VI called *On Priestly Celibacy* (June 24, 1967). You will be able to find it at the Vatican website. You can also look up Pope John Paul's yearly letters to priests, written for every Holy Thursday. God bless.

THOSE SEESAWING ATTRACTIONS

---

dazed and confused

That's what the signer of this letter calls himself.

Hi. I was really thinking about being a priest for a while. Then an exciting feeling came upon me twice and I vowed to Mary and God that I would be chaste, and a priest. I felt great and at peace at the time. Now I feel that maybe I'm being called to marriage. WHAT SHOULD I DO? Keep the vows (though outside of a sacrament) or see if married life is for me? Thanks a bunch!

Dear Dazed,

You promised two separate things to God and Mary. One was to remain chaste, the other to become a priest. However, you were probably thinking of the two in relation to one another. Now, becoming a priest is not just a matter of deciding you want to do it and promising God you will do it; you have to be called and accepted by the Church. So, if for some reason it becomes fairly certain that you are not called to the priesthood, you are automatically free of your promise or vow. In that case you will still have the common Christian obligation to live chastely according to your state in life, which would be true with or without having taken a vow.

I have no idea what age you are, but I am going to guess that you are on the younger side.

You need to speak to someone who knows you well, or who is willing to get to know you, to examine between the two of you if what you felt were just passing feelings or if there are other signs in your life that you may be called to be a priest (or at least if there are no signs that you are not).

When a young man is called to be a priest, the natural desire for marriage does not evaporate; girls don't suddenly become drab and uninteresting and lose their fascination.

What you have to do if you are called is the same as a man who marries: change your behavior, have eyes and heart for no one but the love you have chosen, who has chosen you too.

This takes growing into. That is what seminary formation is for. It takes prayer. It takes personal sacrifice. But it is well worth it.

The priesthood, the special closeness with Christ for whom you have left everything, the total availability to those you are called to help, the ability to take away their sins in confession – these are some of the ways in which Christ pays you back with a happiness very different to what the world can promise you, but so deep and so lasting.

God bless.

seesaw

I'm a rising senior in the university, and I am trying to discern my vocation. My efforts so far seem futile. I oscillate back and forth between marriage and the priesthood like a little child on a seesaw. There are moments when I have the utmost desire to sacrifice everything for the Lord like the courageous saints of our church. Other times, I feel an incredible longing for a Beatrice figure in my life, a woman with whom I can share my most intimate thoughts and feelings. There are times when I'm at mass, though, and I wish I were celebrating it. The gift of 'persona Christi' with which the Triune God uses the priest as an instrument for transforming the bread and wine into the real presence of God Almighty is incredible. Simultaneously, the conjugal act is a cosmic event as well. A man and a woman participate with God in a beautiful act that creates an immortal soul that will outlast all the material universe. Thanks for listening.

Dear Phil,

You feel an alternating, strong attraction to two very good but mutually exclusive ideals. The short of it is that at some stage you are going to have to make a decision. Besides, you seem unsuited to sitting on the fence.

What can I say that might help? Obviously if I were able to tell you infallibly what God wants you to do, you might feel I had solved a problem for you, but I might only have sharpened it, for then you would know exactly which of these paths you were going to have to sacrifice the other for. What you are faced with are two wholly different ways of putting God at the center of your life, two different ways of becoming holy and leaving a positive legacy behind you. The question is not one to ask yourself or me, but Someone else, 'which of these paths do you want me to follow?'

The fact that you are so keenly aware of the value of a true marriage is reassuring. If you are called to be a priest but were to base your choice for celibacy on an aversion to marriage, or a false demeaning of marriage, there would be much lacking – the heart of celibacy, the joyful sacrifice out of love would not be there.

The very fact that time and time again your thoughts are brought back to the priesthood may be significant. There is a spiritual longing that seems to pull you beyond the material. Read Pope John Paul's book *Gift and Mystery,* read the Gospels often, get into the habit of spending some time after Mass considering what a privilege it would be to be the one to make Christ present, and how many could benefit from your priesthood in the confessional. Think of the hearts you could direct and enlighten in your preaching and teaching. As a priest you won't marry or have your own family, but think of how many families will be what God wants them to be through your priesthood, families you would otherwise never have touched...

Think about these things and let Christ speak to your heart. I will pray for you.

---

in my heart...

I inquired at the sisters and they told me to find a spiritual advisor. Since I am leaving school in a month, I have been finding a hard time finding one. In my heart, I feel I am called to marriage. Would it be wise for me to put off dating, since the opportunity has arisen with a really great guy, until I can find a spiritual advisor? Once in confession I asked about vocations, and the priest told me that when I find a great guy or a great order that would really turn me on to Christ, to go in that direction. I am confused.

Dear Marge,

When we say that 'in our heart we feel we are called to marriage' we often mean that we feel much more the pull to marriage than to the vocation. That is not uncommon. As a matter of fact, I am uneasy about a vocation if the attraction to marriage is not also there.

If the thought of a vocation has come into your mind, even though it is facing some stiff competition, it just might be from God. That is what you have to test, and that is why you need to find a spiritual director.

As long as it is possible that God is calling you, I think it would be wise for you to put off dating while you dedicate some more time to God, and do all you can to favor the growth of a vocation in case you have one.

But don't wait for a vocation passively. Find a spiritual director, offer yourself to God in prayer, inquire of the sisters what they recommend that you do in the near future, do some acts of service (pro-life, teach CCD...). All of this will allow you to grow in your heart and in your love.

...an urge, but sometimes...

I have an urge to be a Carmelite nun; I pray about it all the time and hope God will direct me in the right path. Even though I have an urge to be a Carmelite nun, sometimes I feel God is calling me to be a mother, or to the single life. Is this a mix-up of feelings, or is it normal? Please help me. I will continue to pray as usual, Anonymous Please

Dear Anonymous,

All the possibilities are there in your life. So what is happening to you, the urge to be a Carmelite and the feeling you might be called to be a mother, is both a mix-up of feelings and normal. We are all like that; we are full of mixed and alternating feelings, especially as regards a vocation. Why?

The trouble with a decision about a vocation is that it is not as clear as deciding between what is right and what is wrong. In these cases the answer is obvious, you have to choose what is right and do what is good. But as regards the vocation we have to say that marriage and family are good, single life for God is good, religious vocation is good. So which good are we supposed to choose? We know we could do any one of them with God's help, each of them attracts us, so we don't know where to turn and we get confused.

Usually when the vocation comes into our mind and persists there is something to it. It can often be God speaking to us. If you have not done so already, I would encourage you to go and visit a Carmelite convent; if there is one in your city go there often to pray; speak to one of the sisters. Once they get to know you a little they will be able to tell you if it sounds like a vocation to them, and what to do next.

---

two hats

For the last 2 years I have been contemplating joining a religious order. In January of this year, I went to an order for what was called a 'come and see.' I have always been attracted to how the saints gave their lives and everything up for God. And when I turned 22, I felt God was calling me to do the same. After the 'come and see,' I decided that this was God's will and asked them if I could join. I will be joining in June this year.

You would think that I would now be at peace and looking forward to joining the Missionaries of Charity! But no, since returning I have met a really lovely and special guy who shares my love of God and wants to totally give himself to God but as a layperson.

I am very confused. To be honest if you had asked me months ago what was my greatest temptation, marriage would not have ever listed in the top five!! I am becoming increasingly unsettled and I have to say, I am upset that just when I was deciding to go I now have this to deal with. I don't understand what God is wanting of me. I feel guilty that I have these feelings for this guy and this is hindering my spiritual life. It's almost as if I am wearing two hats!!

Please, Father, can you advise me? I have prayed about this and left it in Our Lady's hands, but I would like to have you say some guiding words. Thank you for your help.

My dear friend,

What you are describing is not unusual, and perhaps one of the most natural things that can happen to us. Let's see if I can help you with a few reflections.

To start off, God is always going to keep on making wonderful people – attractive, agreeable, good people. The man you have met is not going to be the last such person you will ever meet in your life, whether you get married or become a nun. The way we allow such people to affect us depends on the direction we have given our life, the options we have taken, the love we have committed ourselves to. When a person is married and somebody terribly interesting crosses her path, she does not immediately think that it is God calling her to make a change. She knows what God wants her to do, and she doesn't let a new person intrude on her life or the commitments she has already made before God. She continues to give herself to her husband and family and lets no one else get close or in the way.

When God calls us to consecrated life, and when we respond, it is just the same. Every attractive person we meet (and a person who is good and virtuous, seeking holiness, is very attractive) is not a sign from God. If you think God is calling you to give your life to him as a consecrated religious, react in the same way as a married woman to all new acquaintances that cross your path. Consecration is becoming Christ's bride.

Maybe what happened was you were looking at your choice as something that you were going to do in the future, not something that made a difference now, so maybe your guard was down. But now you have to make some choices, admittedly hard. You need to go back in prayer and see if all the signs are there that God is calling you to be a nun. If they are, though it will be difficult you need to break with this excellent man because you already have a Fiancé.

Be sure of my prayers.

---

should I turn back or not?

I need to ask this question. I am a temporarily professed sister wondering if this life is for me. I am alternately strongly attracted to the married life and then to the religious. Is this normal, and would it be a mortal sin to leave religious life? Thanks.

Dear Sister,

What you ask is more a theme for ongoing spiritual direction than a one-time, long-distance piece of advice from someone who doesn't know you. Here are some thoughts just to get you going, but I don't want to take your spiritual director's place.

One of the conditions for discerning a vocation is to be normal. Being normal entails having all the facets of our human nature, in its fallen state. Don't be surprised at this last qualifier – it is key.

I would ask you if in your spiritual journey you have taken sufficiently into account that your nature is fallen, and if you do all you can to shore it up with the many aids Christ has given us as Christians and religious: the sacraments (Eucharist and Reconciliation especially), prayer, Scripture, vigilance, penance, apostolate, community life, the practice of charity, the life and example of the founder or foundress, etc. Knowing that what is impossible for man is possible for God, and using these means is the way God has made it possible for us to do the impossible task he gave us.

The process of maturing in our religious vocation is a process of anchoring ourselves always more firmly in God, so that despite all the other pearls that are offered me out there I still choose this priceless one, the vocation he has given me, because I love him and want to serve others for his sake.

Your second question, 'would it be a mortal sin to leave religious life?' does not have a general answer. If you don't have a vocation and leave, obviously there is no sin (quite the contrary). If you do, and still leave, well then the gravity of your action will depend on many circumstances that I couldn't even begin to list here.

But even in the worst-case scenario (that you knew you had a vocation, and still left for the worst of motives), you should never doubt God's mercy. If you are sorry and ask for forgiveness, and are moved to make up for your fault in some way, he will not deny it to you. You may not do exactly what he wanted of you, but he died to save you, and does not repent of his sacrifice; he will do all he can to reach and save the sheep that has gone astray, if that sheep is willing to be saved.

God bless.

SIMULTANEOUS ATTRACTIONS

---

sign I'm not called?

I have been seriously discerning a possible vocation for the past year. One issue just seems to keep giving uncomfortable vibes – lifetime celibacy. Until these little tugs to seriously consider the priesthood started coming, I had always seen myself as getting married and I have dated off and on with nothing leading in that direction. As a layman, celibacy seems easy. You don't feel a sense of permanence to it. Of course, I will surely live it if the Lord wants me to be single. Still as a layman there is always the possibility that someday you may meet a nice Catholic girl and end up getting married. But as a priest, that's it! I am living celibacy and chastity, but I do like girls. How do candidates for the priesthood turn off the God-given attraction of man to woman? If they can't, am I safe to assume the discernment should end right there?

Dear Abel,

It's just as well you are feeling the way you do. It means first, that you are normal; second, that you have up to now been living a good life in the Christian sense; and third, that you have your eyes wide open and understand what is implied in God's call.

If God calls you to be a priest you don't (can't) turn off the God-given attraction of man to woman – we are celibate not because God in some way neuters us when he calls us. Celibacy is a gift you offer God each day. It is something you care for and take care of.

The premise for celibacy and chastity was given by Christ in the Gospel, 'for man it is impossible, but for God everything is possible.' What does a weak man do in order to be faithful to this call and gift?

First of all he prays: this is where the change of heart takes place.

Then he learns to appreciate the gift (by reading and reflecting on what the saints have written about their experience, for example).

He purifies himself by resisting temptation with God's help.

He has a spiritual director and is open with him.

He gives marriage and God's plan for man and woman its proper place – he is not showing his love for God by giving up something bad, but by giving up something good.

He avoids circumstances and situations that will play on his weakness (media, especially, and a certain type of friendship).

He makes sure he stays healthy.

He looks for support from his peers.

He uses his time well.

So you see, celibacy is not something that we 'endure,' but something we give. In its turn it gives great joy and freedom, and is the source of God's blessings on a priest's work. And do you know what else? It shows people you are in the priesthood not for yourself but for them. God bless.

----

both positive and negative feelings...

Hi! For about a year I have been feeling called to be a nun. With this, I have had both positive and negative feelings about becoming a nun. I want to do God's will, but I really stress myself out about whether I am doing it or not. I have always dreamed about being a mother. I know that I would still be a mother to people if I became a nun, but there is a difference. I have also read different pamphlets and books that say the charism of the religious life will be something similar to your own and you will have a passion for that kind of life. I really don't. I visited a convent last month for two weeks and had an awesome time. I deeply admire the faith of the Sisters, but I am not sure it's for me. I also realize that many people run away from God when they are afraid of their calling, and I don't want to do that. Please help! Sorry for the confusing letter.

Dear Dawn,

The attraction to motherhood or fatherhood and the attraction to being a nun or a priest take place on two completely different levels of our life.

Physical motherhood and spiritual motherhood are similar in an analogous way: you can use one to try to understand the other, but they are not on the same level and are not directly comparable. This might be the reason for some of your confusion.

The attraction towards physical parenthood is not just physical; rather, it affects everything we are (emotions, psychology, spirit – everything in us that ranges from the blindly instinctual to the highest sense of self-giving and self-sacrifice).Yet, it is still centered on the physical reality of children. When Christian marriage is lived as a call from God and according to God, it leads the couple through their physical union, their fidelity to God and to one another, their acceptance of life and all the enormous sacrifices that this demands of them, to an ever deeper and more spiritual union where they find the great satisfaction and joy God wants for them.

Our vocation is not a denial of any of the above. A vocation does not mean the above is bad, neither does it mean we are not attracted to it. Nor does it mean that our attraction will somehow magically evaporate on receiving the call.

The question then to answer is: could God be calling me to give myself totally to him despite the other attractions that he himself placed in me when he created me? The answer to this question is always yes.

Our vocation is what he created us for. If we are called, he has placed in us desires that can only be satisfied with the type of love that our vocation implies. It is true that our vocation is spiritual, that it involves a spiritual love and dedication that seem not to have the emotional satisfaction of human love. But that is only what it seems like from the outside. Inside, it is a life of joy.

There is the enormous joy and satisfaction you find in the depths of your conscience when you can go before God with no barriers between you and him; when you know he has asked a lot of you, and you are doing all you can to be faithful to him; when you have given up everything that is dearest to you for his sake.

You also have the bond between you and those who are with you in the same calling: the constant, daily experience of the fruitfulness of your sacrifice; the sense as the years go by of time well spent.

And then you have the very practical ways in which we serve our neighbor – nuns who teach, those who tend the sick and dying, who counsel and encourage, who calm and strengthen, who hold families together. These are all sources of never-ending satisfaction and love despite their difficulty.

That leaves one final question: 'Is he calling me?' I think you should open your soul to him in total trust and say to him in prayer: 'I am short-sighted, I can only see what is in front of me and what I feel. But I trust you. I put myself in your hands. I know that the happiness you have prepared for me in my vocation, whatever it may be, is greater than anything the world can offer. If yours is the narrow way, I want to follow it. Take me.' God bless.

feelings, girls, and heroism

I am 15 years old and considering a vocation to the priesthood, but I am not sure that I am called. I need help discerning if what I feel may be a calling, or just a very good imagination inspired by a bit of religious zeal. The idea of being a priest came from reading the lives of saints who were priests and they really impressed me. The example of a good parish priest I know also helped. The one Saint that sticks out in particular is the Cure d'Ars: St John Vianney, and I have felt a desire to imitate him. But once I felt a desire to imitate St Francis Xavier. Is this just religious enthusiasm or graces pointing me to find my vocation as a priest? Or am I confusing this as a call to better holiness, the call of all Christians?

If you don't mind I would like to expound on these 'feelings.' I feel prompted to become like St John Vianney: become a truly holy youth, enter the seminary, become a priest, and offer the Holy Sacrifice of the Mass, reverently and devoutly. I've imagined St John sitting in the confessional hours at a time, preaching the gospel, teaching his little flock how to truly love Christ and love him better. I am so impressed with him... I think, 'I want to become like him.'

Unfortunately, if these are signs, I've rebelled against them in the past. I had a crush that I let get to my head. I fancied getting married to this girl one day, and just being a good Catholic husband and father, and growing in holiness that way. It got found out and came back to bite me, but somehow I became detached from the idea. I had another short-lived crush on a girl in school, but that didn't last long. Throughout this the idea of a vocation just wouldn't die. I had suffocated it, but somehow it stayed alive and is now stronger. I hope you may be able to shed some light on this. Would you recommend a school for young men considering the priesthood? Thank you.

Dear Peter,

It seems to me that your ups and downs as regards the vocation are quite normal. It would be highly unusual if thoughts of marriage did not come into your mind, and if you did not find girls attractive and even have a crush or two on particular ones. But the priesthood keeps popping back, and the idea you have of what a priest is, and what you would want to do as a priest, is very well-centered. From what you say, it seems to me that it is the priesthood that is attracting you, and not just a general desire for holiness, so I definitely think you should take the matter further. The question is, how?

First, a premise: you are 15, so you are getting more independent but you still are a minor. In God's eyes your parents still have a major, active role to play in your decisions and they have a major responsibility towards you. Granted this, there are schools for boys your age who are thinking of the priesthood, and they can be very helpful for a young man in your situation. However, it is not enough for you to want to go, your parents have to be in agreement as well.

How would you know if this is the way to go? First ask your parents' permission to visit the school, and see what it is like. (Would you fit in? Does it challenge you? Will it help you if you have a vocation...? Speak to the priests who run it, to the kids there; pray with them, play with them, do everything they do for a few days.) If you and the priests there think it will help you, you should speak with your parents about it. Explain why you would like to take this step, have them see the school if they want to. If they agree, go ahead and take the step.

If your parents think it is better for you to finish out high school where you are, then you will have to take very active steps toward helping your vocation grow for the next few years. This will mean going to Mass, Communion and Confession frequently; and having your own favorite prayers as well, especially the Rosary. Now that you know you are made out of flesh and blood and can easily get sidetracked from your vocation by crushes and whatnot, don't be surprised or alarmed if they surface again, but continue to put the priesthood first. Also, try to do something active for your faith in order to spread it to others, be an example for your friends.

I hope these ideas help you, write me back if there is anything else you want to ask or if I can help you in any way. God bless.

PROBLEMS IN CHASTITY

The struggles a young person faces in this area are many and varied, and it is logical to question how they affect the possibility of a vocation. Here are some of the concerns some young people have raised.

---

willing but concerned

Greetings! I discerned about my vocation last year and I was convinced that I want to be a priest, and I am willing to answer that call. The problem is that I can't seem to overcome my sins against chastity, and that I am attracted easily to having relationships with the opposite sex. I am thinking that if I continue with my aspirancy or if I indeed become a seminarian or priest, I might not be able to restrain myself from doing things unbecoming of a priest or seminarian. I love the Church and its priests and I don't want to ruin its name. Right now I am attracted to a girl but am able to restrain myself so far from courting her. I am in college. Do you think I have to think and pray things over again?

Dear Vance,

I am at a distance and do not know you personally, so it is going to be up to you to think over and apply to your own case the points I give you here.

Several things are in place, if I read you well: you are willing to answer God's call if it is to the priesthood, you know the behavior that is expected of you if you do set out on the path of a vocation, you are exercising restraint in the present situation you find yourself in, you love the Church and don't want to let it down.

Your concern arises from two points: your attraction to having a relationship with a girl, and the question of some sins you do not seem to be able to overcome. As regards these, you need to seek the help of a prudent confessor and spiritual advisor. Explain your difficulties to him, and he should be able to tell you if they mean you don't have a vocation, or if they are the normal struggles that can be overcome with a little effort.

As regards the attraction you feel to courting a young woman, there is nothing extraordinary or terribly unusual in that. Keep in mind that as a tendency it will not disappear even if you have a vocation (people often make the mistake of thinking it will). If you give yourself wholeheartedly to your vocation, what you can expect to happen is this: with prayer and the gradual mastery of your imagination, senses and feelings (that you will develop with the help of grace, your own effort and the guidance of your spiritual director), this tendency will not be the only influence on your life and decisions.

As you grow in the life of grace, overcome your habits, become more prayerful and mature as a man—in strength of character—new dimensions will grow in your life. From perhaps being an enormous sacrifice when first we start, chastity and celibacy grow into a sacrifice freely given, and a great source of confirmation in our call.

If your call is to the priesthood, you can be sure that grace will give you all the help you need to put this and your other tendencies in their proper place.

---

weak and struggling

I am slightly confused, and a little sad too. For a while I have been thinking that perhaps God was calling me to be a priest, but I have several problems. I have done some pretty bad things (but nobody knows). I've used the Web to see bad things, and done other things. I went to confession for this, but I just keep doing it; I don't know why. I was just wondering whether this is a definite sign that God would not want me to be a priest.

Dear Greg,

The whole area of our sexual tendencies, and our tremendous weakness there, is humiliating, especially when we know it is wrong and can't figure out why, if we know, we just can't seem to overcome the problem, or even get to the bottom of it.

The fact is, we are weak. The fact is, the devil tempts us. The fact is that having things so easy to access privately, as over the Web, brings out our weakness even more. The fact is, there is tons of this going on around us. How can you pull out of it?

Fortunately, there are steps that you can take.

First you have to pray right. Always tell God why you need his help. Every time you pray, or go to Mass and Communion, tell him that you are too weak on your own to correct your problem, that you need his help. Tell him you need him to change you on the inside so you will want what is right as well as knowing it is right.

Then you really need to get a spiritual director and a regular confessor. Speak with him clearly about the type of problem you are facing. This might be hard to do at the beginning, so if you find it hard to come out and say it, write it down and give it to him to read. Say, 'this is what I want to say but can't.' Once you take this first step the going gets much easier.

The third thing to do is set up a system of accountability with him. If the main reason we fall is our weakness, we need to have something that will shore us up. Be very concrete and focus on what can make the most difference: what you access on the Net, who you cyber with. Take care of this first. Then take care of the other things (your thoughts, etc).

You will also have to look at your activities and how you spend your time. Make sure there is a healthy mix in your day between school, work, sports, prayer, helping others, a hobby that makes you interact personally with others (music or band, for example), involvement in a youth group, etc. The more time you are on your own in front of your screen, the more likely you will give in. Find good friends. Do worthwhile and fun things together. Be busy. A lot of this problem can be just inside your head, and often all you need is some oxygen.

These points will help you get started. From what you say, you seem to have gotten yourself into a bit of a corner. It will take some effort to get out of it, but I do think you will be able to pull things together like they should be and like you want them to be.

VIRGINITY

Several young people wonder if virginity is necessary in order to be able to follow a vocation. The frequency this question is asked reflects the times we are living in, but since the matter is pretty straightforward, there is no need to repeat many questions or answers here.

---

prodigal daughters?

What if someone is not a virgin and has had lots of struggles with purity, but think they probably have a religious vocation? I know of many priests/saints who have had conversions after being like 'prodigal sons,' but don't know of any sisters who have. Could the young woman still become a religious?

Dear Marie,

You are asking a general question, so I will give you a general answer, but I will add also a more particular piece of advice.

The general question is: can a woman who has sinned seriously in the area of chastity have a conversion and become a religious?

The general answer is, of course: yes, it is possible, just like Mary Magdalene converted and followed Jesus right up to the Cross.

The more particular piece of advice is this: Each case has to be looked at with the help of a prudent confessor or spiritual director. Between them they should examine and consider many elements, for example: the roots of the failings, their depth and number, if they have caused an addiction, the depth of the conversion, the results in a person's life (sometimes there is a rejection of men and marriage because of an abuse suffered – that would have to be healed first), and so forth.

When these points are considered, it may well turn out that in a particular instance the most prudent conclusion is that God is not calling that person to the celibate state.

is it a requirement?

Do you have to be a virgin to enter the priesthood or religious life?

Dear Ambrose,

It is not an absolute requirement, but if a person has fallen, it is necessary that he have picked himself up, be living chastely, and show by the control he has over his passions that he is now able to live celibately.

Some young people lose their virginity without knowing there is anything really wrong with it because 'that's what everyone does,' only to realize the truth afterwards – often with shame and horror. Others might have gone deliberately against their conscience. Both cases are different, but both require conversion, and conversion might come more easily to the first than to the second. After conversion both will require humility and an effort to be faithful.

If a man is no longer a virgin, he has to ask himself what caused it. To enter the seminary, it is necessary that he be decided to live chastely and celibately. However, that is not enough; he must also give certain guarantees that he will be able to do so with God's help. He therefore must be willing to apply all the necessary means to be faithful to his decision (prayer and self-discipline; conviction that it is his calling; and a healthy, Christian outlook on life, relationships and marriage).

He must have a realistic view of himself, to see if he really can live the celibate life with God's help: for example, the case of a man with one occasion of weakness a long time ago is very different from someone who until recently has been plagued with frequent difficulties and concessions in this area.

A FREE COMMITMENT

Although this is not in answer to a question, I'll add it in here in case it can be of help. It is a promise that puts into words several of the points we have brought out about chastity, celibacy and freedom in the previous pages. It is the outline an individual seminarian can use to focus his thoughts in this area, live realistically, and then use and adapt when he becomes a deacon or priest.

Lord Jesus:

You chose for yourself a life of celibacy. You did not marry and you dedicated your public life totally to the work your Father gave to you to do.

I take you as the model for my priesthood. My whole body, soul, heart and mind will be for your Church and for those people you have entrusted to me. I therefore commit myself to live celibately and chastely in mind and body, always.

I know this promise is more than I can do on my own and in my weakness. I know it entails sacrifice not only of what is base, as you require of every Christian, but also of many good things you gave to us in creation, in particular the love and support of a wife and the fulfillment of having my own family.

I also know full well that the culture I come from and in which I will be your priest is aggressively sensual and sexual and will play upon my weakness.

In order to prepare myself to live a life of celibacy I take upon myself the following commitments:

• I will be a man of prayer. Over and above my liturgical duties as a seminarian (priest) (liturgy of the hours, Eucharistic Celebration and Communion) I will dedicate _____ hours/minutes to prayer (spiritual reading____, meditation ___, adoration ____) each day, every day.

· I will be a true son of Mary and express this in my daily rosary.

· I will invest my time well and wisely:

· in my prayer,

· in the exercise of my ministry,

· in my study and preparation of my preaching,

· in necessary rest and exercise.

· I will be extra-careful in the use I make of the media, eliminating all frivolity, time-wasters, and especially all that would be just titillation and veiled sensuality. I refer especially to TV, movies, books, magazines and the Internet.

· I will be circumspect and prudent in my dealings with women, especially teenagers, young women, and those married women whose marriages are going through difficulty. I will only meet them in appropriate places, where my actions can be seen by others. I will not hug or touch them in any way other than a handshake. I will keep in mind especially that, 'whoever looks at a woman with impure desire has already sinned in his heart.'

· With children I will remember that 'if anyone leads astray one of these, it were better that a millstone be tied around his neck and thrown into the sea.' I will do all I can to bring them to Christ, and provide a ministry that will cater to their innocence, curiosity and energy – but I will never touch them, be totally alone with them, or allow myself to get emotionally attached to them. I am aware that Christ's standards in this are much higher than the world's.

· I will foster healthy friendships with fellow priests, fostering mutual support, spiritual and pastoral enrichment and cooperation, and relaxation.

· I will remain close to my own family, but not to the detriment of my ministry or vocation; neither will I intrude upon them, but respect each one in his own call and obligations.

I take upon myself these commitments as a means to an end, as an aid to my priestly chastity and celibacy. I also want to make this virtue into one of the main means I have of living and proclaiming in my life your words, 'seek first the Kingdom,' and, 'what good is it to you if you gain in this life at the cost of your soul?'

I take these commitments because you have put it in my heart: you have called me to be your living witness in this life of the glory and happiness you have in store for us in the next.

I take these commitments freely, in joy and in hope, because I want my love for you to be total, unhampered, and effective. Amen.

CHAPTER FIVE

Signs and Signposts

We know a vocation must be sensed inside us; there must be something inside pushing us. It has to be a personal decision. But at the same time there is something rather reckless in the following of a vocation, so there has to be something that confirms this internal feeling and tells us there is more to it than a mere 'gut feeling.' Then there are the external signs that are subjective in nature, which we will address briefly in the second part of this chapter.

WHAT ARE THE SIGNS OF A VOCATION?

what signs are they looking for?

I have heard it mentioned in a few places that when a person is in the process of being interviewed for a religious community, those who are already in the order will look for the appropriate accompanying signs of the call to religious life in the person. Could you please tell me what these signs would be?

Dear Terri,

There are general signs that are common to all vocations, and then specific signs that tell if you are a possible candidate for a particular group or order.

The general signs have to do with physical health, psychological health, maturity proper to your age, intellectual ability, spiritual health and a spiritual motive.

The specific signs are the general ones as they apply to a particular group with its own standards and requirements, and any additional requirements they might have that relate to their specific charism and apostolic work.

Just to explain very briefly the general signs:

· Physical health means normal health for a young person, with no physical condition that would keep you from fulfilling habitually the normal duties and responsibilities involved in the particular vocation you are considering.

· Psychological health means the same, but applied to your psychology: ability to weather the normal stress involved in the vocation; freedom from illness, addictions, psychosis, neurosis, or obsessions.

· Maturity proper to your age is connected to a certain degree with psychological health: to have the ability to discern, a functioning conscience and will, independence from peer pressure, and emotional stability. Obviously you would expect more in this regard from a mid-twenty-year-old than from a seventeen-year-old, so that's why we say 'proper to your age.'

· Intellectual ability. Since in most vocations you have to take college studies, you need to have the necessary ability, but that is not true of every vocation, so you should ask the group you are interested in.

· Spiritual health. You usually need to have acquired a certain stability in your spiritual life, though you might still have your struggles. This means that you are not too recent a convert, not given to strange devotions, that you give God his place, and have an active faith in the Church as Christ founded it.

· Spiritual motive. This means that in looking into the vocation, you are motivated by something more than human convenience or ambition – a desire to save souls, to use your life in the most pleasing way to God, to bring God's mercy to others, more concern for what you are called to be than what you are called to do.

Particular groups will have also their own requirements as regards age, studies completed before joining, etc.

Terri, I hope this helps clear things up somewhat for you. It is very brief, I know, but you will probably be able to connect it with your own experience.

---

how can you tell?

How is one supposed to know if God is calling him to priesthood or not? This is probably one of those questions that can't be answered specifically, but with a round-about answer, which is okay, but I need some kind of answer.

Dear Carl,

One thing you have to keep in mind (and it's amazing how often we forget it, but it certainly brings us a lot of peace) is that, if God is calling us, he is definitely going to give us enough signs for us to recognize the fact – otherwise he would be very impractical for someone as intelligent as he is!

But another truth is this: it's a call, not a kidnapping. Since he is interested in our love, he is not going to force us. There you have the whole problem.

Now what types of signs does God usually send to the person he calls?

First he gives them the natural qualities that are needed for the particular calling he has in mind – of course, we have to do our part and develop them: health, intelligence, ability to relate to people, etc.

Then he gives the supernatural qualities (faith, hope, love), which we also have to develop.

And finally he supplies some trigger, something that makes us ask if we are called, something that will open our heart and mind to the possibility of a vocation. It can be the example of a priest we know, the suggestion of a friend or teacher – any number of things, even the thought itself that one day pops into our mind and makes us ask the question).

From there on out he expects and needs our cooperation. We have to put our energies into it.

What should you do now? Continue to develop your life of faith through prayer and the sacraments. Continue to learn more about your faith by reading books that will help your faith mature from feelings to convictions, truths that you can live by and to which you can turn to find your way. Then do something new: take a step. Talk about your thoughts to a priest you trust – he will ask you about yourself, your health, your faith journey, your past, and your answers will help him to give you advice. He will be able to tell pretty soon if you should not pursue the priesthood. Then, visit a seminary or check out a religious order you might have heard about and are interested in. Take care, and happy searching!

---

any signs towards the sisterhood?

As tempted as I am to simply type in my name and say, 'hey, what's my vocation?' I know it's not that simple. But are there any signs toward the sisterhood? I'm very confused.

Dear Angelique,

As regards signs for the sisterhood, there are some – but beware, they are not infallible. Let me explain:

In order for you to have a vocation there are certain conditions you have to fulfill: starting from the bottom up, you have to have the necessary physical health for that vocation, the necessary psychological and emotional health, the necessary intelligence, and a maturity that is proportionate to your age.

All of the above doesn't make you 'extraordinary,' just pretty normal. It is the human base that is needed for a vocation, so if there is anything missing that you are not able to acquire by putting in a little bit of effort, it would be a sign that you don't have a vocation.

The final condition, if all the above are in place, is the clincher: you have to be interested in the vocation for a proper reason. It would not be enough of a reason to want to be a Sister in order to travel, or in order to teach, or in order to take care of the sick. These are human reasons still on the natural level, even though the latter two are highly commendable goals.

Your interest should be faith-motivated: to care for the sick, or teach, in order to love Christ by serving others, for example; or in order to use your life in the way most pleasing to God; or in order to save your own soul....

The big sign for me is that you are asking yourself the question. That can often be God speaking to your soul, moving you, gently leading you to look into it more and open yourself more to his grace.

If you have the basic conditions I mentioned above, it would be well worth your while looking into it more. Visit a congregation of nuns that interests you. Or look into the consecrated life in one of the new movements in the Church. Get to know the people there, go on a retreat.

And, especially, ask yourself a question that is much more important than: 'is God calling me?' Ask yourself: 'am I willing to say Yes if he is calling me?' Sometimes that's the problem.

---

psychological testing

Hi there! I am in the middle of discerning a call to priesthood. In previous responses you mentioned that a series of psychological tests have to passed or gone through. I am no psychopath by nature, but this kinda gives me the creeps! What exactly does this mean? Can you give me some idea of what to expect? And please pray for me! Many thanks and God bless!

Dear Drew,

I'll be glad to pray for you. You seem like most young men who are called to the priesthood: regular and normal.

You are probably in good health, and you have intelligence enough to at least handle college courses since you are in college now. Nevertheless, when you apply to the seminary you are going to be asked for doctors' certificates of good health and transcripts from your high school or university. Psychological testing is in the same vein. It is just to make sure of what is most probably already evident to anyone who knows you: that you are normal for your age in character, emotional maturity, and personal identity. Forget about the couch and the swinging watch on a chain, merciless probing into the depths of your unconscious, or whatever else may spring to mind. What you usually face are some standardized written 'inventories,' and an interview with a psychologist based on the results of the written material.

Psychologists who interview for seminaries usually believe in grace and place a high value on morality – so if you have been living your faith and behaving yourself you will not be dismissed as maladjusted or in need of therapy.

SPECIAL SIGNS: GOOD OR BAD?

---

bargaining with God

A good friend of mine told me he dreamt he was prostrated in the sanctuary for the Sacrament of Holy Orders. He wants to try the seminary but is afraid. At times he is very keen for marriage too and is confused. He told me he has asked God for a simple sign and has set a deadline for it. Only God and he know what the sign is. The moment I heard how he is trying to do to discern his vocation in life, personally, it sounded wrong to me, and he may end up with his mind playing tricks on him. I told him to approach a Spiritual Director to discuss it, and he is not in favor of the idea. I am more than worried for him after hearing that he decided to work based on signs. What can I do to help him?

Dear Audrey,

It is very worrisome that your friend has decided to pursue the path of asking God for concrete signs. Jesus himself said, 'an evil and perverse generation looks for signs,' and he said this not because he didn't want them to know the truth about him, but because they had already received lots of signs and still wanted more.

It is best, I think, to tell your friend that you are afraid he may be blinding himself, closing his eyes to the signs God has already given him. In that case what he is lacking is not signs but the generosity and faith to act on them.

Tell him to read the beginning of Chapter 5 in St John's Gospel (the curing of the man at the pool). When Jesus told him he was cured and to get up, the man had no proof except Jesus' command. He only received the proof when he actually did what Jesus told him, when he actually tried to stand up and found that now he could. It is the same when we feel a vocation: we find out it really is from God when we take steps to follow it.

Your friend really needs a spiritual director (and maybe a tough one).

---

a voice...

I come from a big family, and I always thought that it would be nice if one of us became a priest or a nun. When I was little my family were very active members of our church because my mother used to work in a convent. I was born on the birthday of a missionary sister, so I'm not sure if this was just a coincidence or God was trying to tell me something. I always wanted to grow up to be like one of the people who gave catechism classes: I admired them and wanted to be like them. I wanted to be close to the Church and somehow be an active member. Until recently I never thought of offering my life to God. But now I'm having thoughts of becoming a nun or somehow serving God, but I'm not sure what my real call in life is. When I was getting confirmed and the lights were dimmed, I was near the altar and I heard somebody call my name, when I turned there was nobody around the altar except Jesus in the cross, I'm not sure if this was a calling or I'm just hearing things. Please help.

Dear Samantha,

I can't tell if it was just your imagination or not, but I wouldn't give too much importance to it anyway. What matters most here is the gradual development that there has been in your life, the constant attraction you have had towards giving your life to God, especially once you brought prayer more into your life.

So I think you should put yourself in God's hands every time you pray, and begin looking into various religious orders. Start with the one you are most familiar with, and see what happens. This will give you much more to go on than any other feelings or signs that you can't figure out.

SPECIFIC PROBLEMS AND SITUATIONS

recent personal conversion

Would anyone ever be turned away from the priesthood for something they had done in the past, if they had a true vocation and had been living a moral life for the past couple of years?

Dear Adrian,

Your question uncovers a facet of vocation that may not be easy for me to explain or for you to follow, but I'll try.

You ask about past faults and if someone might possibly be turned away from a vocation because of them 'even if they had a true vocation and had been living a moral life for the past couple of years.' It is helpful to dwell on this, because it is the same as asking: Can I be turned away even if I have a vocation?

Here is the essence of a vocation: it is a call. We don't choose, we are chosen. Even when we think we feel a vocation, we have to find out if God is really calling us, if what we feel is true. God chooses, we only answer.

Serious sin in the past can affect a vocation. It can in some instances be an impediment, and it might indicate clearly that God is not calling a person to religious or priestly life. I have no idea of the nature of the failings you are thinking of, and to find out if what is bothering you is an impediment, you would have to speak personally (do so in confession if you want) with a priest you trust, and accept his advice.

You may find out that what you did, or its effects, is an impediment, and yet still yearn to be a priest. This is where your faith has to come in and you have to understand that even though you are generous enough and would like to serve God as a priest, he is not actually calling you.

Granted, this is sometimes hard to accept. We tend to think the vocation consists in me wanting it, but that's not the case. It is God calling me. Sometimes we don't feel like it and he still calls, other times we want it and he doesn't. In one case and the other we have to trust him and accept what he says.

I fear the betrayal...

My question regards my own vocation, and how to discern what my vocation is. My life took a sharp turn back to the Church some years ago, and since then I have wondered about my vocation. My problem is as follows: In all my life (I am now in my 20s) I never had any thoughts about the religious life, nor did anyone ever introduce me to it. In other words, my heart has always been set on marriage, and in fact seems to have been married all this time to the prospect of having a lifelong female companion. In addition to this, my lifestyle before my return to the faith was a typical Catholic male's life in the '90s, (not necessarily virtuous). So as you can see I am somewhat conditioned from the start. When I came back to the faith, I separated myself from contact with women, and began to seriously think about the religious life. And so, now I wonder what to look out for that may lead me to either state. I fear the betrayal of the religious life, while at the same time I fear the sacrifice of marriage. Aside from giving it time, what is prescribed for those in my position?

Dear Rob,

The fact that you never thought of the priesthood before your return to the faith is of no importance in finding an answer to your vocational question. God has his time for everyone.

What does have more of a bearing is your life while away from the faith. You will have to speak very frankly to a priest or spiritual director about your past life in order to see if it is in any way an impediment to the religious life, or if it would simply make it imprudent for you to attempt living it.

If you have been through no more than the normal struggles, then the next step would be for you to start looking around, and visit the community that attracts you.

As regards your two fears, the fear that you might betray the religious life through your weakness is healthy and necessary. When you speak to a priest, as I just mentioned, you can examine with him the basis of your fear, and find out from him the way to grow in strength with God's grace and how to protect yourself from your own weakness. Your fear of the sacrifice of marriage may be healthy as well; it may help you to be prudent in choosing the right person, but you should not let it paralyze you. You should definitely not go into religious life just because you are afraid of the commitment of marriage; you will find the commitment of religious life no less demanding and it comes without the intimate companionship and some of the human consolation that marriage offers.

---

just came to the faith

I know that vocations are open to converts to the Church. But, I wanted to know if there was a prescribed time period that has to elapse following the convert being fully taken into the life of the Church before he could be considered as a candidate for the priesthood, for example?

Dear Enrique,

The Church does require that a prudent period of time elapse after you enter the Church before it accepts you as a candidate for the priesthood. Usually it is at least a year and a half. The various orders and seminaries may have different policies in this regard, and you would have to contact each one for their own procedures.

One of the reasons for the suggested waiting period is to make sure that the conversion is sincere and stable and that the 'vocation' is a true call and not just the flush of conversion. It takes time to see that. Also, you can be sure that when you apply to a seminary they will look at more than just the time you have been in the Church.

---

baptized Catholic, but not brought up in the Church

I was baptized in the Catholic Church as an infant but was not raised in the faith. Now as an adult I am 99.9% sure that I am going to return to the Church. Now for my question. I think I may have a vocation. When I contact the priest at my local parish, when I return home from business, should I tell him this also? Should I find a spiritual director now or wait until I am confirmed?

Dear Don,

That is wonderful news! Congratulations!

There is nothing wrong with telling your priest your thoughts from the time you contact him, and it would also be good for you to find a spiritual director even before you are confirmed.

It is important, though, to separate the two matters: your coming back to the Church, and your vocation – they are two separate, different graces (although one—your coming back—is the source of the other: your vocation). If you were to discover you don't have a vocation, it ought not to impact in any negative way the fervor and commitment with which you return to a life of grace, the sacraments, and apostolate within the Church.

Hi! I'm a Protestant, but I was baptized in the Catholic Church. I have always felt a strong calling to a vocation, but being Protestant I don't know what to do. My grandparents on my father's side are Catholic and I was baptized in their church, but I attend my mother's Protestant church since my father does not attend church any more. If you could answer my question it would be greatly appreciated.

Dear Laura,

I think what you are feeling is an open invitation from Christ to start searching out your Catholic roots. He may be calling you 'back home.' He wants you to be closer to him. The Catholic Church is centered on Christ, who is really and personally present in the Eucharist.

If your grandparents are still living they may be able to start explaining the faith to you. If not, you can start by asking questions to the apologetics expert at Life on the Rock or on other good Catholic web sites. You will find many people more than glad to give you materials to read and help you along.

If you have a vocation you will find out as Christ draws you closer to himself. Offer yourself totally to him from now in prayer.

THE QUESTION OF AGE

how young?

I need to find out info for a Christian Living class. I am a senior in high school, 17 years old. The assignment was to find out a fact about one of the different lifestyles or vocations. I would like to know, if possible, if there are any religious communities that accept young women into formation at a young age like 17. What is the process they require?

Dear Julie,

Seventeen is the minimum age for entering the novitiate, which is the first stage in any religious institute. Usually age is not the only factor, so when you get in touch with them they will take into consideration as well your physical and psychological health, your maturity considering your age, if you are inquiring and want to enter of your own free will, and the studies you have completed (usually at least the 12th grade).

There are some groups that have a pre-novitiate program where you can do your high school while living a structured life that will prepare you for the novitiate, but you cannot formally enter until the proper age.

If a young woman proves satisfactory in the areas mentioned above and is seeking entry for a proper motive, there are some communities that will accept her straight out of high school, while others will require that she get a college degree first. You have to ask.

---

how old is old?

I will be confirmed into the Catholic Church this Easter vigil. I'm in my 30s and single; I know beyond a shadow of a doubt that God is calling me to the religious life. I know there is a place for me somewhere, but in watching some programs, I'm very concerned about my age. Can I get into a brotherhood at my age?

Dear Kevin,

Once you are received into the Church and are confirmed you will have over a year before you can be accepted into a seminary or religious order, so it would be wise to use that time to deepen your understanding of the grace you have been given in your conversion, and to visit places where you think God might want you to serve him.

First ask yourself if the Holy Spirit is leading you more in the direction of contemplative or active life, and if active, to service at home or on the missions. And trust in God's providence.

The vocation director of your local diocese is sure to have on hand a booklet describing different religious orders of brothers. Ask for one and read through it. As you look around, God will put you in touch with the religious family he wants for you.

Pray often. I do not think your age will be a problem, but that is up to each group you get in contact with to tell you, since their admissions policies vary.

SPECIFIC SITUATIONS: SIGNS FOR OR AGAINST?

---

full disclosure?

I am in college, and I am in the process of discerning a vocation to religious life. For the past year, I have been talking with one of the priests I have known for years who also happens to be the vocations director for my home diocese, and I really feel God is calling me to become a religious sister. This priest has supported me through all this and believes I am sincere and has helped me. About three years ago, I was going through a really rough time, and I found that my father had been bookmarking porno-graphic web sites. They became like an escape for me, like a fantasy in my mind to escape my life. It made me feel worse and worse until I felt I didn't even want to live any-more. At that point, I got really scared and turned back to God for help, made a good confession, and got my life straightened out.

Later, I ran into the vocations director, and I have been talking to him since. It was like one thing sort of led to another and I can't help but feel the hand of God in all of this. I haven't told him about what happened, because it is so hard for me to talk about that because I now hate all that stuff so much, and I feel really bad about doing all

that stuff. I guess my question is if I should tell him about
it all.

On the one hand, I feel almost as if I should tell him
because it has had an effect on who I am, and I almost feel
like God couldn't possibly be calling me to the religious
life because of all that stuff, and that's something I'm
struggling with right now. On the other hand, it has something to do with my father's reputation, and I've already
confessed it and been truly sorry for it, and I know God
has forgiven me for it, so I feel bad about bringing it up
again.

Dear Christine,

Your question is simple, and it boils down to this: Do I have to
have 'full disclosure' with the spiritual director who is helping me
discern my vocation?

First, though, let us consider the problem you had. It seems you
have put it behind you, having confessed it, made up your mind to
change your habits, and followed through. So on the surface it
would not seem to be an out-and-out impediment to religious life.
Nevertheless, it did indeed take place, and it tells you something
about yourself.

You will have to mention it at some stage (not all the details,
but just as much as you have said here) at least to the person who
is ultimately going to be responsible for accepting you into the religious order you want to join. You can understand why. It is part of
the whole picture of yourself, and that person needs to know it in
order to give you reasoned and sound advice as regards entering
that vocation.

As for telling the spiritual director you have now, while it is not
absolutely necessary, he will probably be able to help you more if
you do. He will be better able to tell you if it has a bearing on your

vocation, he will put it together with everything else he knows about you, and will prudently examine if it changes anything with respect to your vocation.

Concerning your father's reputation, I do not think it is necessary to mention him as you explain what happened. It would be enough to say that you found these sites bookmarked on the computer without saying who did it. However, even if you did mention it was him, neither your spiritual director nor the person who interviews you for the order will speak to anyone else about the incident, so it will not go beyond them, and your father's reputation would not be affected .

anxiety and depression

I am a young woman contemplating a religious vocation. A few months ago, I was turned down for a vocation retreat when I told the particular community (contemplatives) that I had a mental illness. It is a social anxiety disorder, the effects of which are taken care of for the most part by medication, so I live a very ordinary life now. If I am being called to the religious life by the Lord, I feel that it may be to a contemplative community. Is such a call, if any call at all, impossible? Is my illness a sign by God that I am not called? I would be willing to follow God's will either way.

Dear Michelle,

There are several elements that need to be taken into consideration in searching for an answer to your question. You have to consider the nature and depth of the illness you suffer from, the nature of the medication (and its secondary effects), your doctor's prognosis, and the particular policies of individual orders, to name the most obvious.

You must also consider the fact that if you suffer from a social anxiety disorder, there is at least the possibility that the silence and prayer of contemplative life might seem like a very attractive relief to you. From the outside it is difficult to realize just how demanding the contemplative life is, and it requires pretty robust mental health.

I would recommend that you gather full information on your condition (mostly, the points I mention in the first paragraph above) and then speak over a period of time with the vocation directresses of several contemplative convents. If they all tend to dissuade you from pursuing the contemplative vocation, you can be pretty sure that this is a sign from God that it is not your calling. If any of them do encourage you, make sure to tell them that other convents have tried to dissuade you, just to be honest and get a balanced opinion.

---

good health

What is considered 'good health' by the 'average' congregation? I know that a serious illness would contraindicate a calling to religious life. For example, let's say someone has high blood pressure that is under control with medication. Would the 'average' congregation consider this 'good health?'

Dear David,

The matter of health has to be taken in context. What each order will consider 'average health' will be seen in relation to its specific spirit and apostolate, and the various practical commitments entailed in each one's way of life. Also, with the help of medication, many conditions that in the past would have ruled out religious life, or a particular kind of religious life, may no longer be a problem nowadays.

That's a general answer. Now, to get more specific, if you have a medical condition and want to join a particular group, no matter which one it is, you need to get to know them. Once you have gotten to know them and think it may be the place, bring them information on the exact details of your condition. They will examine its nature, consult as regards the side effects of any medication you take (both long and short-term effects), and obtain a prognosis to see how it may affect your ability to live their life in the future. Based on what they see, they should be able to come to a conclusion and give you an answer, and possibly make some recommendations since, if your condition rules them out, it might not necessarily rule out the priesthood.

---

bills

I feel called to be a religious. The only thing holding me back is bills I must pay off. Is it possible to still enter? Have any others discerning vocations had to wait because of bills? I leave it all in God's hands. It just seems to take so long to pay them off.

Dear Albert,

I have met quite a few young people who are in the same position as yourself. Their most common mistake is to hold off making a decision on the vocation until after they have paid up their bills.

You need to make a firm decision in favor of your vocation, and then go all out to pay off your debts, even if you are not exactly sure whether to go to the diocese or join a religious community, or which community to join.

If you make the decision, then your needs change, and most probably your expenses, allowing you to save more and faster. You probably will not need to spend so much on extras: if you are renting an apartment you may be able to move back home, you might have things you can sell off, you might be more willing to take a second or third job since you won't need to socialize as much.

The key thing to do is say to God and to yourself: 'yes, this is it, it's you and nobody or nothing else in my life.' If you become passive and just wait to see when you can pay them off, you will waste precious years.

If you don't know exactly where God wants you to go, use all the time you can finding out, and when you find the place that may be it, you can ask them about your debts. It could be that they can help you arrange something as well.

---

taken to drink

Father, I have read nothing on you yet, I am going to write this with zero knowledge on you so that I may be able to hear what you have to say with no feelings, good or bad, towards you. I am a senior in college, graduating in December. I come from a wealthy family who is Catholic and religious. I drink a good amount with my family and friends and do not think that it is possible to get out of that trend, because everyone I know, including my family, drinks a good amount as well. I have always felt a pull towards the priesthood, however my personal doubts, including my sins and my inability to achieve well in school have left me to not really pursue this possibility in my life. I know I want to do something good for people with my life, but I am not sure what is going to happen. Whatever you get out of this please let me know, however it is a bunch of jumble so I'm not sure that you will be able to get anything out of it.

Dear Jacob,

From what you say, you feel a pull towards the priesthood but have never acted on it for several reasons, among them: your personal doubts (you do not say if they are doubts about yourself or about your faith), your sins (I don't know if this is connected to what you say about your drinking habits), and your difficulties in school-work. What you are sure about is your desire to do something good for people in your life.

There are obviously things that you know you have to work on in your own life so as to be in a position to do what God wants of you as soon as you find out what it is. I would recommend that you start by getting more order into your life – begin with setting aside some time each day for prayer (go to Mass more frequently), and if you think you drink too much, begin to set yourself some reasonable limits. Then you need to get someone who can help you more personally, a kind of spiritual guide. I think a retreat would also be a helpful step for you since it would give you time to reflect and clear up any doubts arising from your past sins.

These points should be enough to start with. Be patient, one step at a time; let me know if you think you can begin by doing what I mention above. And be sure of my prayers.

---

fear

Hi! I joined a religious group, and they recommended that I take some time outside the convent, though my formators are willing to recommend me to another congregation. That was years ago, now I am 30 and I live a healthy life. The more I am with people, the more I felt so much love and the longing to share that love to all. I have so much fear about entering religious life, though I feel so much inclined to that state of life. My reasons: 1.) What if my health fails; I easily get sick? 2.) What if again I am not permitted to continue? 3.) My father is so much against my entering the convent, and I don't want to frustrate him. I am so confused. What should I do?

Dear Tara,

You are now 30, and you have behind you the experience of trying religious life and being told to take some time outside the convent. The result is a continued desire to live religious life, although mixed with fears which have to do with your health, the possibility you may again be told not to continue, and fear of upsetting your father.

Start by eliminating the least important. If you are 30 and what you want to do is good, your father's reaction is the least important to worry about.

The other two fears should be addressed and settled by speaking to the vocation director or superiors of the congregation you are thinking of joining. Ask them what they think. I imagine you have stayed in touch with them, so they should be able to give you concrete advice. If they do not think you should join their group, ask them if they think you have a vocation at all and if you should look into some other order, or if they think your call is to the lay state. Then take them at their word and go on what they say. If they have doubts, you can safely conclude your vocation is to the lay state.

Don't forget to pray and offer yourself to God, and ask him for the fortitude to accept whatever it is he wants you to do.

---

bad habits, addictions

Would an unhealthy bad habit/addiction that someone has tried unsuccessfully so far to quit, e.g. smoking or smokeless tobacco, impede someone from being considered for the priesthood? I don't think I would put these on the same level as alcohol or other drugs which affect the mind and senses, but it is still an addiction.

Dear Joel,

Of itself something like smoking would not be an impediment for following the priesthood. There is certainly a huge difference between it and an addiction to drugs or drink.

However, it is right to ask if there might be a fundamental flaw in a person who has this or some other light addiction, something of which the addiction is only a symptom, and something that would make it imprudent for that person to take on the commitments of a religious or priestly vocation. It will not be so in every case, but in some it might. Some people are just a bundle of nerves, and there seems to be no other way for them to handle themselves than through some outlet like smoking. Sometimes smoking is an escape from an underlying problem or unresolved conflict. At times it can be a sort of subconscious will to self-destruction. I won't get into all of that and other possible causes because I am not qualified.

Let me just tell you something I have learned from experience: quite often a teenager smokes out of the natural drive for independence that, funnily enough, drives him to imitate his friends and become a fashion fiend. He finds plenty of support in acquiring the new, difficult habit (smoking doesn't come as easily as acquiring a liking for chocolate; it's expensive, and it has no practical advantages), but once the addiction takes root, he doesn't find the same support to break loose from it.

Many are trapped in it despite their desire to quit, like the many who suffer from overeating. What they often lack is real purpose to break free. But once they have a purpose (a vocation for some, or the preference of the girl they really think they might want to marry, or the condition for a job they really want, or a health scare) they have been able to quit, and often cold turkey. Positive support and doing things that will take their mind off it often helps them on their way.

I think I went off on a tangent, but I hope it helps. If smoking is not a sign of a major unresolved issue in a person's life, he should be hopeful. All he needs is a reason, and then he has to bite the bullet.

how smart?

How smart do you have to be to be a priest? I am in community college now and not doing terrific but am passing. I am worried that I might not do well in the seminary. But then maybe it is because I work about 20-25 hours a week and in the seminary will I have more time to study and not work?

Dear Peter,

To be a priest you ordinarily have to be able to handle college studies. The time you put into work each week now is probably a factor that's preventing you from 'doing terrific.'

When you get into the seminary you may not be able to put all of those 20-25 hours into study. You will have other responsibilities and will probably dedicate more time to prayer, but you will have more hours for study than you have now, you may be more relaxed, you most probably will have fewer distractions, and you will find greater motivation to do better.

Don't be afraid of the studies. If God is calling you, you can do it with an extra effort. You may even surprise yourself. And remember, studies are only a means to an end. They are not your goal in life.

CHAPTER SIX

Going Beyond Discernment and Signs: Making the Decision

THE GENEROSITY QUESTION

---

a soldier for God?

I'm torn between joining the military or the priesthood. It's confusing because it seems like I should join the military and get married. But at the same time, priests, sometimes not even after five minutes of meeting me, are always telling me I should be a priest or at least hinting at it. 'Yeah, you should be a soldier for God.' And the idea sounds totally logical to me. I read your book 'Peter on the Shore' and agree with all the points it makes especially forsaking oneself for the cause of Christ and I love the whole concept but... I can't tell if the vocation just isn't for me or whether I'm just afraid. I am confused about my future and feel I am somehow letting God down by my lack of faith. I even feel somehow guilty just reading the lives of the saints, especially St Ignatius of Loyola. Please help me decide what kind of soldier I should be. Thank you.

Dear Philip,

It seems that your confusion stems from the fact that while everyone seems to see 'priest' written all over you, you still would love to join the military and get married. Before getting into the matter any further let me tell you that I cannot say that you have a vocation. The most I can ever say is if someone has the usual signs of a vocation. The only real way of telling if you do have one is by following it if the signs point in that direction. When Peter stepped out of the boat, he did not know for sure if he could walk on the water or not, but he trusted Jesus enough to take the first step; and even then after he had done it for a while, when he began to think about what he was actually daring to do, he got nervous and began to sink—and he had to turn to the answer to everything: 'Lord! Save me, I'm drowning!'

So, a certain amount of insecurity, second thoughts and fear are not to be unexpected when you let Jesus start calling the shots in your life. He goes a little too fast, a little deeper than is comfortable, he asks a little more than we would like, and the only guarantee he gives us is his word.

But there is really only one way to follow Jesus, and that is totally.

Ask yourself these questions to see where you stand: Do you think that the thoughts you have, the fact that you can't seem to drop the thought of the priesthood, the fact that others seem to see it in you – do you think that all of this is just a human thing or maybe God is saying something to you through it all? What would you do if you knew for definite that he wants you to be a priest, would you leave everything and give it 100%? Would you like to know if he is calling you (are you prepared to take the risk that he might be)?

If you think there is a possibility God might be behind this, and you are willing to take him at his word (or his suggestion), then you need to sit down with a priest you trust and open your whole life to him. Let him in so that he can examine your life with you and see if there is any sure sign that God is NOT calling you. If there isn't, you need to take a deep breath, step over the side of your boat, put your feet on the waves and start walking; and don't, don't take your eyes off him.

As for the desire to get married and your military career, they are NOT a sign that he is not calling you. They are a sign that you are normal, and if he is calling you, that you are going to follow him out of love and not by default. God bless.

generosity

Hi, I am confused right now because while I feel God is asking me to open my heart to religious life, it is the last thing in the world I would ever have chosen for myself. I first felt a calling when I heard a vocation story told. I cried all night about it; I was absolutely devastated by the thought; it was as if God was asking me to give up my entire life and everything that I love.

I have talked about it with my spiritual director, and she counseled me to be open and just give God a chance – that he may only be asking for my generosity, and that if I do have a vocation that he will supply all the joy I could ask for.

My question is: Are people with vocations really happy or do they just convince themselves that they are? And is it a sin for me to be so upset about God possibly giving me such a wonderful and beautiful gift? I honestly do believe that a vocation is a wonderful gift. I just don't want it.

Dear Kristin,

You're wonderful! You've put your finger on something significant. I think you have put into words what a lot of other readers are thinking and going through, and I am sure they are thanking you right now for saying it so clearly and honestly. I just hope I can answer in a way that will help you and them.

First off, you have to understand how we are made. We are much more in tune with the world around us than with spiritual things. Through our senses we see, hear, feel, touch, smell, talk, enjoy all those things that go on around us. Anything else seems too abstract and not really real. That is why when all our friends are going to a certain movie and our parents say we can't, we don't readily see why: we just want to do what everyone else is doing and have fun with them.

But when we start considering what is right or wrong, honest or dishonest, we enter into a new dimension of reality, and sometimes it means we part ways with people we thought were our friends. As we mature humanly, we put less emphasis on what our senses and feelings tell us, and what is right and good becomes more important in our lives.

On top of this our faith brings us into a completely different and new reality, far beyond the grasp of our senses. If you have faith, you know that what you receive in Communion is not bread but the Body of Christ, and even though you can't see or taste the difference, you treat it differently, you adore it because it is Christ really present.

Our faith tells us the truth about our life, why we are here on earth, what matters, what is most important, how Christ has loved us. But the big problem for us is that we don't reach faith through our senses. A chocolate sundae is always going to exert a certain appeal that any abstract spiritual principle, no matter how beautiful it might be, just cannot seem to match in the same way. That is just the way God made us.

Now let's get back to your question. What you are in the middle of is the struggle we all have of letting go, putting what pleases our senses into perspective, realizing that there is another dimension to happiness that is much deeper than what appeals to us superficially. We can't imagine there is more than what is immediately evident to us; it doesn't make much sense to us on first impression, though our faith tells us otherwise.

So I would say that what you are going through is not primarily a struggle with a vocation, but the struggle involved in maturing spiritually, in beginning to put Christ in first place, and practicing trust in him that he is all that matters, that he will give us true happiness. No matter what your vocation is, you have to cross this threshold in your life. (A married person promises to love the other 'for better

and for worse, for richer and for poorer, in sickness and in health.'
Aren't we talking about the same thing here?)

And so my advice is: don't focus specifically on the vocation
now. Read the Gospel and tell Christ that you want to get to know
him and love him. Ask for this grace. It is the center of our faith, and
the only real problem we have to solve. All the rest will take care of
itself once you begin to get to know and love Christ. Then you will
discover happiness and peace in your conscience, and you will
taste what only he can give.

THE COLLEGE QUESTION

Quite a number of young people ask about the need for college,
and the topics range from the purely speculative to the eminently
practical. Some questions are valid, while others are due to mis-
conceptions either about the vocation itself or what one studies in
the seminary. Here is a sampling. I hope that the reflections will be
helpful for you in making up your mind.

---

theology before seminary?

I have been very seriously considering the priesthood
lately. I'm going to be a senior in high school this next
year, so I have a while before I can actually enter the seminary if that's what God's call for me is. I want very badly
to get a degree in theology before I enter any vocation, but
especially the priesthood. Would or could I acquire this
degree while in the seminary, or is it something I need to
do on my own? Also, if I were to go to the seminary first,
would I be able to get the degree after I became a priest?

Dear Misha,

Seminarians usually get a college degree before studying theology. In most cases you can get your college degree while being in the seminary or house of formation, but there are some dioceses and orders that require you to have the degree before you start in the seminary. From the point of view of your priesthood and the studies you will do in theology, it is best to major in philosophy in college, but not any philosophy. Go somewhere you can study systematic philosophy, sometimes called perennial philosophy; or, at the very least, do the Great Books course.

You will study theology in the seminary, all seminarians do, and at the very least take what corresponds to a bachelor's degree.

You are right in wanting to study theology well; it is nonsense to think we have anything to offer people if we haven't opened our heart and soul to God in prayer and our mind to him in study. Once we have done that, we can apply all our strength to loving him and serving him in preaching and extending his Kingdom.

---

college experience necessary?

I have left the question about becoming a priest or religious open for a little while, but I always thought that I was expected to go to college to gain life experience before applying for the seminary. I'll be a senior in high school this year, and I was wondering what I should do. Should I go to college first or should I start discerning my vocation before running off to the university? I would also appreciate it if you could give some advice on discernment.

Dear Phil,

It is not essential to go to college before entering the seminary. There may be some individuals for whom it might be good and even necessary to do college first, but my experience is that they seem to be the exception.

Nevertheless, there are seminaries and religious orders that for their own reasons require potential candidates to do college before entering. They usually provide some sort of support program for their candidates who are doing college.

So, to answer your question: don't just plan on going to college and figuring out your vocation later. Try to use your senior year to get an answer and make a decision.

Use your senior year to take major steps in your openness to God. Keep up your prayer life, ask God to help you always put him at the center and to look at your life in terms of what you can do for him and for others.

Use your senior year also to get information. Start from where you are right now. Are you initially attracted to diocesan priesthood or to religious life? Is there any particular diocese or religious order you know about that attracts you? Get in contact with them, and see where it leads.

You seem to be thinking of a vocation, or at least are open to it, and you express yourself well, so presuming everything else in your life is as normal, I would be inclined to think that you may be dealing with a vocation here. Find yourself a spiritual director. He will help you sort through and tell the difference between reality and feelings, and he will give you light if you get confused with too much information on too many seminaries.

If at the end of the year, you have seen you may have a vocation, and are pretty sure of where you should go, you will have solved the question of college. If the diocese or order you want to join accepts you straight out of high school and your spiritual director does not see overriding reasons not to take the step, then go ahead and start in seminary without going to college first. If the diocese or order prefers you do college first, then do college, try to resolve the financial implications, and keep your focus on the priesthood. This will save you from wasting your time in college and from getting sidetracked from your vocation.

A final word as regards life experience. The real experience we want to gain from life is to form the strength of character we need to be true to our convictions. Any other experience is more harmful than helpful. You do not have to go to college in order to gain this positive maturity. You can get it in the seminary too, and a good seminary will place a priority on your human maturing. As a matter of fact, given that we are weak and are easily influenced by others, the experience the unwary accumulate in college is often of the harmful type that is better done without.

---

what college studies would help my vocation?

I am still in the process of discerning my vocation (prayer, talking with my confessor, etc.). I have begun my search for colleges and need some advice. I just want to choose a school where I can take courses and study things that will help me in my vocation. Because of my parents, I have also considered just finding a public university with a good campus ministry program. This whole thing is just really confusing. I was wondering if you have any advice about schools I could look at.

Dear Caitlin,

You are a junior, so you still have time to work with, but here is something to help you along.

First thought: if already now in high school you think God might be calling you, it would be good to inquire into orders or movements that accept candidates directly out of high school, rather than put off your vocation until after college. I would recommend this if you are reasonably mature for your age and relate normally to others, socially speaking.

Then, as regards colleges: I do not know about the campus ministry programs at the public colleges in your state, but if you know a good priest, ask him for advice on where there is a good program.

When you are thinking about a vocation it would seem that the logical subjects to take in college would be religion or philosophy, but you already know that it depends entirely on where you go and the professors you have. Not all philosophy that is taught is reliable, and not all theology is respectful of revelation, grace, and the role God gave the Church as guardian of his truth. If you really have to go to college and it is a secular college, pick subjects that are helpful but where you won't have to face your faith being attacked day in, day out. If you go to a Catholic college pick your teachers well and take philosophy, Great Books, or theology.

------

have my cake and eat it too?

Next year will be my senior year in college. For the past few years, I have felt at various times an attraction to the priesthood. I have been in contact with my diocesan vocations director and through my contact with him and my spiritual director, I think that I might have a vocation to the diocesan priesthood.

However, I am a music major and love music very much. I would like to get a master's degree in music, and I know that if I go into the diocesan priesthood, it will be much more difficult to do so. I'm not sure that I will feel like my music education is enough with just an undergraduate education. Is taking the year or two to complete my master's degree before I apply to the diocese trying to have my cake and eat it too, or is it a reasonable way to develop the gifts that God gave me at the most suitable time? Thank you very much for your time and ministry.

Dear Seeker,

To attempt at answering your question, I am going to have to do some supposing. You mention that you have been in contact with your diocesan vocations director and that this has led you to think that you may have a vocation to the diocesan priesthood. I am going to suppose that he is in agreement with you, or has not raised doubts as regards your conclusion. And I am going to suppose also that you really mean 'think' and not just 'feel,' in other words that it is not just a vague feeling that you would like to be a priest, but that through your discussions with him you have come to a conclusion that seems well-founded and has reasons behind it. In still other words, with the vocations director you have examined the priesthood, your own itinerary in life, your own abilities and spiritual dispositions, and God's action in your life... and your joint conclusion is that God might be calling you to the priesthood.

A second set of assumptions I am making is that the only reason you are hesitating in making your decision is your love for music, and the feeling you have that if you don't get your master's you may regret it, since you most probably may not be able to do so in the seminary. I am presuming you are not in debt after college and are free to enter the seminary right away, and I do not know if the same would be the case if you did the master's.

With all those presumptions and assumptions out of the way, however, I am still not going to answer your question directly. Wanting to do your master's may be to want to have your cake and eat it, but there is a more fundamental question that you have to face: what place is music going to occupy in your life as a seminarian and as a priest? Is it going to be first place, or is your music going to serve a purpose? Music and music ministry are great means to express and educate what is in our heart, but as a priest it is definitely inferior in importance to your prayer life, to your theological education, your ability to preach and counsel, your need to visit the sick and be at your parishioners' beck and call for their spiritual needs. Then you also need to consider and ask yourself about the use of your time. We will only live so long, only God knows how much exactly, so: if you are called to the priesthood, do you want to reduce the time you can serve Christ by the years it will take you to do the master's? And here we come to what I consider a major point in making these decisions: 'a priest is not his own' and we can never make a really mature vocation decision as long as we are at the center of our considerations. So, will it be better for the people who need you to wait the extra years it will take for you to complete your studies?

So, finally, my answer is this: the Master is at the door and calling you. If to do what he wants you to do as a priest, you are going to need your music master's, the opportunity will arise for you to do it after you have said yes to him; if not, then don't worry. Either way, follow him now.

---

catch-22

I'm going to be a high school senior this year and am just about certain I have a calling. There is an order I'd like to join straight out of high school, but their age limit is 21. It only stands to reason that I'd spend the time before I'm 21 going to college. But, student loans will hinder me from getting in. What's a boy to do?

Dear Boyd,

It does seem a real catch-22: you can't enter until you are 21, but if you go to college your loans will not allow you to enter when you are old enough.

First, look into all the different provinces of the group you are interested in; there may be a variety of policies, and some province might accept you before college.

Generally, religious orders that have minimum age restrictions such as you mention are aware of the type of problem you face and have tried to work out some solution. Some have programs that you can enroll in that are almost like a candidacy – they tell you where you can go to college so as to live with the community on or off campus. By living with them you can grow in their spirit and also keep your debts to a minimum, and you avoid the other distractions of college.

Some groups will tell you what to study in college, and if you follow their advice and are accepted by them when you are old enough, they take care of the loans after you get ordained.

You have to inquire and do your homework.

FAMILY MATTERS

Let us start with a cry that comes from the heart of a young girl: Why does following a vocation mean putting the family in second place? It comes from a sensitive soul seeking to understand what God is doing to her family.

---

why do they take you away?

This question might be kind of odd, but I was wondering why is it that when you become a sister they take you away from your family and barely ever let you see them? I have two older sisters. One entered a convent three years ago August, and another is entering this August. Each left right out of high school, and I will be the last girl in the family. Troubled and Confused.

Dear Troubled,

Your question is not at all odd. It stems from the fact that we tend to judge everything as it relates to us personally, and we react to everything according to how it affects us personally. This is much more so when we are younger, and only with time and when we mature and learn to love do we overcome this natural tendency.

You feel like your sisters have been 'taken away,' and 'are not allowed' to visit you. There is the hint here of the thought that since they really love you, somebody must be stopping them from seeing you, not allowing them, for they couldn't possibly really want this themselves.

It is easy to forget that they have followed their vocation and given themselves to God, choosing him freely and exclusively, out of love, even at this price.

They feel the separation too, yet they have chosen him. And think of your parents – how they must feel. Yet they have given your sisters at their young age freedom to do what is best for them, what God wants them to do, and they (your parents) didn't try to stop them.

It is impossible, especially if you come from a good family, not to feel the separation. So what can you do? Say that God is cruel, that some religious orders are cruel? No. What you have to do is ask God to help you enter into a new dimension in your life, where you grow out of seeing everything only as it relates to yourself. That is what growing up means, humanly and spiritually. You have to let your faith help you understand what is happening.

What are some of the things that your faith tells you about your sisters' vocations? It tells you God has called them. It tells you our time on earth is to do good for others. It tells you that Christ made immense sacrifices to give us eternal life, and if we love him we will offer ourselves to do the same.

I hope these reflections help you. You will discover others as you bring your thought to Jesus and speak with him after Communion.

Maybe, too, part of what you feel is the uncertainty of what it will be like to be the only girl, perhaps the only child, at home. Make sure you don't mope around. Get involved in things that interest you, that will help you grow, and in which you can help others. Talk this over with your parents.

---

parents willing, but I'm the only child

I have been looking at a religious vocation for quite some time now. I have been praying and I began talking about this with friends and some of the sisters at my parish. However, I still do not know what is the best thing for me to do. My parents want to support me but it is very hard for them. I am the only child. I feel guilty at times, but I feel drawn to give my life to God. How will I know that this is, without a doubt, the best thing to do?

Dear Molly,

It seems to me that some very important elements are already in place as regards your vocation. You feel drawn to religious life, it is not a passing fad for it has lasted some years, you have been praying, you have been inquiring, your parents are extremely generous for, even though you are an only child and it is hard on them, they want to support you. I would imagine you have been trying to develop your relationship with God.

There is another question you need to ask yourself and find an answer to: of the different ways of giving yourself to God (religious orders, consecrated life in a movement), is there any that has caught your attention or attracted you especially? Is there any person you have seen and thought, 'Maybe God wants me to be like him or her?' If there is, I would think you now need to visit them, and start talking to them about their particular life and charism, their requirements for entrance, etc. This will give you much more of an answer as to what to do now than your own speculation.

One note of caution, though. You seem to be looking for mathematical evidence, an absolute sign of what is best to do. You won't get one. The most you will get is that you use your head, your faith and your heart, and when you put it all together it isn't as crazy as it seems, but it still takes faith.

---

my parents have other expectations

For some time now, I have been considering a religious vocation. Every day is a struggle. I strongly feel this call, but there's a problem. I know that we must do God's will, but there's a part of me that doesn't want this call. Sometimes I just want to run and hide. I think this is because my parents are expecting something else of me. I've told two friends and a priest. I know that they are all trying to help, but I'm confused as to whether or not to continue with this.

Dear Jean-Marie,

It seems to me that you may be in the beginning stages of a vocation, and the struggle you are facing gives you an advantage over many other young people I know who are considering a vocation.

Very often the first steps in a vocation are made in joy and enthusiasm, and people can get the idea that not having problems and living on an emotional high are the true signs of a vocation. So, conversely, they think problems mean you don't have one. That doesn't make sense because we all have problems.

There is always a part of us that resists, hollers and objects – at least if we are human. That should be a premise in all our searching. A vocation is always on weak ground until it meets difficulties.

In your present situation, one thing—the main thing—to do is to foster your relationship with Christ. Give him some time each day; read the Gospel, visit him in the Eucharist, fill your mind and heart and soul with all he has done for you. Ask Mary to show him to you. Let your love for him grow in a simple and direct way (work on overcoming your shortcomings and failures, any bad habits you might have), until you can sincerely say to him: 'You are first in my life. I only want to do whatever pleases you most.'

This might sound too simple, but the day you can say it from the bottom of your heart without any reservation whatsoever, you will for all practical purposes have solved your vocational dilemma.

You mention your parents' expectations for you, at least as far as you can detect. Often parents do not bring up the question of a vocation in case their child thinks they are trying to force them. At some stage (exactly when depends in part on your age and how soon you want to make a move) you should talk with them about it.

The other little signs (nuns seem to be 'popping up' everywhere, for example) to me just mean you are sensitive to the idea. They may be a remote sign at the most, not much more. Don't give them great importance.

---

my parents think I am being pressured

I have been considering a vocation to the priesthood. I attend a Catholic high school and have had many discussions with my chaplain. I attend Mass every morning before school and work on many projects with him. I have tried to talk to my parents about my feelings, but they don't understand, and sometimes get angry with me for doing the good things I do with my chaplain and with the youth group at my parish. They believe that my chaplain is pushing me into the priesthood, and that's not the case at all...

Dear Tom,

From the information you give here, it seems there is much reason to think God may be calling you. It is good that you are in touch with your chaplain and talking to him about this. As he gets to know you better, has you work on projects, sees how you do with the youth group at your parish, he will be able to give his advice regarding your vocation. God doesn't usually give more signs of our call than the 'inner voice' (our thought that, 'maybe') and an 'outside voice' (someone else, like your chaplain, who can tell that it is not our imagination).

Your main problem seems to be your parents' reaction. Their suspicion that you are having the vocation pushed on you is frustrating. Of course. One good result is that you have really examined yourself and seen that it is not someone else forcing you, just you wanting to do what God wants of you.

What you should do under these circumstances, and how you should obey the fourth commandment—which tells us to honor our father and mother—depends on your age and on the advice of your chaplain. When you are a minor, honoring usually means obeying; as you get older it means holding them in respect, but not shirking what your conscience shows you is your duty.

If you are still a minor, you can insist with your parents, but if their answer is No for now, then you just have to stay put geographically. By that I mean you won't be able to go away to a seminary. But you can still move spiritually: grow in prayer, in your work with the youth group, in your knowledge about the vocation. Examine if God is calling you to diocesan priesthood (like your pastor) or to a religious congregation. Visit seminaries. Prepare the way.

If you are old enough to make a step this summer, then get ready for it – unless your chaplain sees something you need to work on before joining the seminary.

---

my mother wants grandchildren!

Hello there. I have had 'inclinations' towards religious life for the past four years, and I started serious spiritual direction almost a year and a half ago. I have been in general discernment this whole time getting ready for vocation discernment. And, even though I am not in formal discernment, I am really starting to get a sense that I may be called to religious life. I also have this desire to completely surrender my life to Christ, not only in my daily life (which I do already), but in everything I do. My spiritual director is aware of this, and pretty soon we will be going into vocation discernment. However, the conflict comes in with my mother. The reason my mom hates the idea (for the most part) is because she wants grandchildren. I know that I will eventually get to this conflict with my mother in spiritual direction, and ultimately I have to trust in the Lord, but if you could provide any advice or input, I would appreciate it.

Dear Libby,

There is only one piece of advice I can give you: keep your priorities straight. If you put God in first place, everything else will work out for the best. It may take a long time (these things usually do, since we are talking about real life here and not a TV show) and the attitudes that we are up against are deeply ingrained.

The main thing you can ask God for your mother is not that she accept or understand your vocation (from what you say it would sound like you may have one), but the gift of faith. Faith will help her not only in this instance but in the many other difficulties we must face in life.

---

what is best for my family?

Hi. I have been discerning a vocation for about a year now. I have such an amazing desire to be a bride of Christ. I want to give Him every part of me. I think that I have a vocation to religious life. My question is: How can I know when the right time to take a step in applying is? There is an order I visited; my heart longs to go. However, my family is going through a lot right now. My parents are depressed and argue constantly. I love them. I have talked to them about entering. They are not exactly excited about it. That's okay though. I have a certain peace about it. I just wonder how I can discern whether waiting would be good for my family.

Dear Penny,

When you say you are away at school, I presume you mean college, so that would mean you are no longer a minor. Since you are already talking to a vocation director, I also presume that you have not been told you are mistaken in your attraction to be a nun in that order, and you have gone into certain detail about yourself, your situation, your background, and your spiritual development with her.

If you have been open with the vocation director and she has not seen anything that you need to work on before entering her order, it would seem to me like the time is now.

Your lingering doubt is in regards to your family. You have to be realistic there. You cannot solve your parents' problem for them. You may in some cases be able to help, but that's about it. They have to work through it themselves.

In most cases what most helps parents and families going through their normal difficulties is the clear example of one of their children or siblings who knows what is important in life, and goes for it wholeheartedly. Unless your parents' case is extreme, your example, and then your prayers for them, which I am sure will be constant and plentiful, will help more than your physical presence.

CHAPTER SEVEN

The Problem of Choosing

BETWEEN CONTEMPLATIVE AND ACTIVE

---

is the contemplative life selfish?

I spoke to a parish priest whom I have known for a long time. When I explained that I was trying to discern between a contemplative or a more active apostolate, he told me that he thought that a strictly contemplative lifestyle was selfish and self-absorbed, and that I needed to get out among the people to do anything of value. I reminded him that many of the great Saints were cloistered contemplatives. But he thought that these are different times which call for people to use their voices and their skills out in society. I suppose that many people do not see the value of the cloistered contemplative lifestyle. I still feel a pull in both directions. On a given day I think that I would be perfectly content to worship God in a contemplative lifestyle. Then on the following day when I am reminded (e.g. by listening to the slanted viewpoints on the evening news) of the very serious moral problems present in our society, I feel that maybe God needs more people to do something active.

Dear Mary,

Don't worry, the contemplative vocation is not only a valid way to give your life to God, today it is of especially vital importance for the Church. You don't have to have a contemplative vocation to know and appreciate that.

The active vocation is necessary today not because it is more important than the contemplative, but because the Church is a body, and each member has a different function to fulfill. Each member needs all the others. Laypeople need religious, actives need contemplatives, and the contemplatives need actives so that their prayer will have an instrument so that it can bear fruit.

Continue as you are going, putting everything in God's hands, and doing all that depends on you so that his grace will have something to work with.

The search will purify you and will allow him to speak to you more clearly. He knows what he wants you to do.

---

which is more useful?

My plans for my life were to get married, have a family, and to continue working in my profession. However, I discovered that God had other plans for me, and I believe I am called to religious life. I was not happy about this at first, but through prayer, daily Mass, and visits before the Blessed Sacrament, I have developed a clearer picture of God's will for me. I am now very grateful for his call, since I realize his love and mercy toward such an imperfect being as myself. What now remains is to find out where I am to serve him best. I believe very strongly that the U.S. is a country hard hit with moral and spiritual decay, and also a country which sets an example (i.e. movies, TV) for the rest of the world. Therefore, I believe that the U.S. is in great need of healing, which can only occur with an awareness of, and a turning towards, God. I am trying to figure out if I can best help in a contemplative order (i.e. through prayer in reparation to the Sacred Heart of Jesus), or through a more active apostolate (i.e. actively

spreading the gospel message in the U.S.). I am torn; do you have any insight on this?

Dear Marilyn,

I agree thoroughly with what you say about both the spiritual needs and global importance of the U.S. The impact of the U.S. on the world—the culture we export—makes it most urgent that we heal ourselves at home, renewing everything we are with the light of Christ in his gospel. Only then can the presumption to be a shining city on a hill ring true, and only then will we have something to give.

That is going to take a lot of work by a lot of people on many levels. We need the prayer and sacrifice of contemplatives. We need the hands-on work of the active religious, from the compassionate healing of those who care for the sick and infected to the dedication of those who educate. We need the priest in the confessional and the priest in the pulpit, the personal commitment of parents to the formation of each one of their children, and the commitment of lay Catholics in all walks of society to conduct themselves first and foremost as followers of Christ.

Where you fit in, the work that has been reserved for you, is a very personal discovery. Christ already has it in mind, but you have to discover it.

The only way to do that is to start from where you are. You see two needs—both of which are real, and both of which must be addressed—so you are not going to be able to figure out the answer by simply asking which is best to take care of.

Pray to the Holy Spirit for light. Tell him you don't want what is easier for you, but what he leads you to. You really do need the help of a spiritual director. And you need to visit the places you are thinking about in order to give the Holy Spirit a chance to speak more directly and clearly to your soul when you visit each place.

how much does a priest pray?

Regarding the priesthood, how much time a day in, let's say, a large parish, does the parish priest get to pray? The reason why I ask is because I'm probably going to enter seminary in a couple of years, after I finish college, and my prayer time is very important to me and it increases daily. Quiet time as well, by myself, in front of the Blessed Sacrament is a must.

Dear Toby,

The answer is: it depends on the priest.

In pretty much any parish, large or small, as also in any apostolate that is not parish work, you are always going to find there is much more to do than you have time for – especially if you are really trying to serve your people. So your work will naturally tend to encroach on other important things in your life – notably your prayer.

What you need to build up is personal discipline, a habit of putting first things first, the conviction that the usefulness of your priesthood is based on how alive Christ is in you. I know many busy pastors who never miss their holy hour first thing in the morning. Most say it's what keeps them going.

A prudent spiritual director will help you discover the proper balance in your life in terms of the actual amount of time to spend in prayer each day, and the type of prayer you do. Time before the Eucharist is time well spent, especially when we pray with Mary and go to the Scriptures.

You are on the right track.

BETWEEN THE DIOCESE AND RELIGIOUS ORDERS

what's the difference?

I'm a college student discerning a possible vocation to the priesthood, and I was wondering how and when one should find out with which order they should become affiliated. I'm especially wondering about the discernment of the diocesan priesthood vs. non-diocesan orders? (for example: the teaching orders – the local Church benefits from their schools).

Dear Vince,

When you wonder if you are called to one or the other, you have to ask yourself what God is putting in your heart to do in order to serve the local Church – where are you attracted to? Religious priests live in community, have a particular charism, live under a rule of life, and have to be willing to be sent where they are needed. Look at the gifts God has given you – are they leading more towards community life, or towards a particular type of ministry? Then you should also look at whatever God has put in your path: his providence puts what he wants you to do in your path. A very good way to get some light is to visit the seminaries of the places you are interested in. God bless.

where am I needed?

Suppose one has a deep calling to one of the legitimate religious orders that exclusively offer the Mass and sacraments in the Tridentine Rite, yet the need for priests in his own diocese is very great. Does one follow one's deep calling to the Tridentine Rite order where he will be serving a comparatively small number of people, or does he forego this calling to serve in his diocese in the Novus Ordo on a much larger scale, where the need is so great?

Dear Jon,

Your question gets right to the heart of what a vocation is. It is not what we prefer, what we like, but where we see God is leading us. You have to search in your soul for the answer to your question. If despite your deep attraction (I think this is a better word than 'calling') to a legitimate religious order that exclusively follows the 'Tridentine Rite,' the Holy Spirit is moving you to consider and address the larger needs of the Church, it may well be a sign of where God wants you to be. You have to make the premise of your search that you want to do what he wants, not what you want. And then you have to be prepared to draw the conclusions, to give up what you are attached and attracted to (no doubt for many good reasons) if he asks something else of you, and not look back. Be sure of my prayers.

BETWEEN ONE RELIGIOUS ORDER AND ANOTHER

---

so many options

I am pursuing a call to the religious life. In doing so I am rather overwhelmed by all my options. I am very pulled toward the Franciscan way of life, but I would feel much better if I could make a more informed decision. My question is this: What are the differences between Franciscans, Dominicans, Benedictines, and Carmelites (and any others I might have missed)?

Dear Sheila,

I've got to admit I'm stumped. I couldn't explain in a short space (or even in a long one) the difference between each and every order – those you mention and those you missed. Fortunately, I don't think it is necessary in order to help you.

A vocation is not a question of an 'informed decision' in the sense that we have checked into all the options and choose the one we think is best.

The only 'informed decision' we need in a vocation is this: I feel an attraction towards a certain form of life, there is a particular group that interests me or I heard about, in your case the Franciscans, so I go check them out. I visit, learn more about and experience the charism that God gave the Church through St Francis, and while I am there they get to know me.

After I experience their spirit and they check me out, if both they and I are still interested (in other words if I think and they agree that I may be called to their way of life), that is information enough to focus on them; go deeper in your discernment without spending time looking at other places.

If you are initially interested in more places than one, then check out each one, but there is no need to go hunting down more and more places to visit. A major part of your 'informed decision' will take place during Novitiate, when you will go deeply into the vocation you have been called to. That way, when you take your vows you will be fully informed of what God expects of you.

grew up with one order, attracted to another

My question is regarding how to know where it is God may be asking me to pursue my vocation. My family as well as myself are very involved in a movement associated with an order of priests. And it was through this involvement that I first acknowledged the possibility of a vocation and began to discern. The only thing is that I now feel very drawn to a different order because of their charism and particular forms of worship. I love the order that I was raised in, but I don't have the same spiritual passion as I have for the other order, and so am confused as to how to know where it is I should pursue this. I know how much my parents and everyone else hopes I will consecrate my life in their movement. All your thoughts are appreciated!

Dear Rebecca,

I am sure that the only true concern your parents have is that you do what God wants you to do.

While the most natural and common thing would be to give yourself to God through the lay movement that has nurtured you up to now, this is not set in stone; God can just as easily call you somewhere else.

What you need to do is make sure that you stay close to God in prayer, and offer yourself to him to use you in whatever way he sees best for his Church. Then you have to do some simple and mature examination of yourself in order to test the attraction you feel for the other order and make sure it has the signs of being from God. Make sure it is not only an attraction to some externals (the habit they wear, for example), but a deep attraction to their spirit and charism.

For example, the movement you are in might use charismatic prayer, and the order might be more contemplative; the movement may have a variety of apostolates, and the order might have just one focused mission, let's say teaching. Each group may have its own particular way of living poverty.

These are just some examples, but the point is that if you have a call to another order, you will have to leave behind certain things that you have been nourished on up to now and which seem very natural to you, and maybe even seem to you the only way to do things.

You should not try to bring those things you love with you, or judge the order according to what you are used to in the movement. It is going to take a lot of detachment, perhaps more than you imagine, to learn and accept fully into your life a new charism.

You should think about this, and if you have a calling, that will be God's will for you and he will give you the grace.

I HAVE SEARCHED AND NOTHING SATISFIES ME

---

start my own group?

I have felt called to religious life for about a year. I have investigated many religious orders hoping to find one that was of interest to me. Although different aspects of these orders were interesting, no one had all that I am looking for. Is it silly to think that I could, after much discernment and questioning, found a new order with other interested men?

Dear Sean,

Everything is possible, and God can choose any way he wants to do his work. So it is not a totally silly idea.

From what I have read about the founding of religious orders, it is seldom the case that the founder examines the scene and comes to a rational, clear, perfectly reasoned decision of what is needed and then sets about applying the very specific idea of which he is totally sure. It seems that the inspiration comes unbidden, usually to the perplexity even of the founder himself. Often the foundation is started 'unintentionally,' being an informal group that then gels. When steps are taken, it always seeks light and confirmation from a spiritual director and then the Church itself.

My advice would be to perhaps leave the eventuality of founding a new order on the back burner for now and examine your approach towards your vocation.

If you have felt a call to religious life for more than a year, and you have concentrated your search on finding an order that has exactly the ingredients you are looking for, I think it is time to adjust.

Get the help of a spiritual director so that together you can examine your motives and the importance of the things you are looking for in an order, to see if they really bear the signs of God's inspiration or if they are trivial. (For example, a certain color of habit is trivial – spiritual life is substantial.) That may cause you to reexamine some of the conclusions you have already come to.

From there on out, there is not much I can say to you. You and your spiritual director will have to take it as it comes and figure out which way God is pointing.

---

they say everything is going to change

Hello. For some time I had been considering a vocation to the priesthood, but now that I am in college (freshman year at a Catholic university) I have heard some strange things that are changing my mind. Our campus ministry priests seem very certain that the priesthood will change soon after we get a new pope. Supposedly there will be married priests and women priests. Anyway, it all sounded suspicious to me until I talked over Christmas with a parish priest at home and he said that there will 'indeed be changes' to counter the priest shortage, and that we must act in the spirit of Vatican II. I am very confused, not just because of this but because of a lot of the stuff that goes on in school. The Masses in the chapel don't even seem like Mass, like when they teach us to say the Our Father AND MOTHER. Is the church really changing like this? It doesn't seem right. Anyway, what is the point of me going into the seminary now if this all really going to happen? Are these rumors true? Please offer any advice you can.

Dear Jonathan,

These people are not living in the real (Catholic) world. Thirty years ago they were saying the same; that after Paul VI another Pope a little more sensible would come along and change his teaching on birth control and celibacy.

Steer away from those who can damage your faith. Get your guidance from priests, religious and laypeople who are not busy telling God what he has to do, but doing what he wants.

Don't let anyone rob you of your faith. Study the Catechism, read good books and listen to tapes that can provide you with the answers. (St Joseph's Communications and Catholic Answers are two good sources.) Get your friends interested in their faith and listen to the tapes together and discuss them.

Go to Mass often, and when you receive Christ in Communion, tell him you want to serve him and be a light for your brothers and sisters. He will strengthen you, and lead you.

---

how can I tell if a particular group is OK?

I am considering a call to the religious life. I have looked into a few congregations so far. A woman I spoke briefly with about this warned me about staying away from certain orders since she believed they were not being true to the teachings of the Church. I don't want to get involved in something that is merely following current social ideas and trends versus being truly grounded in Christ and the Church. When I visit a congregation, how could I tell?

Dear Angela,

To some it might seem either disloyal or paranoid to ask the communities you visit regarding their fidelity to the Church. It is neither.

There are two reasons to ask the question: One is the nature of the problems that religious life in general has gone through in recent decades. The other is less circumstantial and more basic: you are simultaneously a rational creature and a believer (you can only be a believer if you are rational). It would certainly be a mistake to reduce your faith to only what you can see with reason, but it would be no less a mistake to give yourself to a vocation unthinkingly.

As regards the vocation: you believe that Christ is calling you to a specific community, and you believe that they are worthy of your trust, that they are doing what Christ intends for them to do – and, therefore, if you join, you will too. No matter what community you join, if they are faithful to their charism and you apply your mind and your prayer to absorbing that charism into your life, you should experience the wonderful joy of discovering the deep roots it has in the sacraments, discipline and teaching of the Church. This is your reason and reflection at work.

Now, to answer your question. Let me start with a simple truth and a warning. The simple truth is there are things so obvious they should not be denied and cannot be argued around. Like the emperor with no clothes; everyone, even the simplest can see so.

That's the truth, now here is the warning: It is also true that 'a little learning is a terrible thing,' and we live in times in which some have set themselves up as judges of others while lacking the necessary knowledge or balance for such an endeavor. While we should not be blind to the obvious, we should be careful about setting ourselves up as judges.

There are certain elements that the Church in its teachings has consistently said are essential to religious life: prayer, community life and some form of religious habit as a sign of consecration. When you visit a community these should be readily visible.

Other points to look for: how central is the Eucharist to the community's life? Is there a sense of obedience, service? Is there joy? Do they believe in the cross? How much prayer is there?

Ask them about their founder, if they follow his or her rule? Do they do the apostolate they were founded for? Is there a sense of communion with the Church? What do they think of the Pope?

Ask about the formation process too (e.g., how long, what stages it is made up of). If they take studies, where do they do them.

These and similar questions will let you see more than just 'if they are with the Church,' but they will also help you to see if it feels like home to you – a necessary ingredient if God is calling you there.

---

doubts about my home diocese

First off, how can someone become a good, loyal priest to the Church when the diocese he wants to go into is liberal? My home diocese is very liberal but I want to be here because my family and friends are all here.

Dear Ed,

Your question is a thorny but very practical one.

First you have to be sure that your impressions about your diocese are true. For that you need the counsel of a prudent and knowledgeable priest. Make sure you are not extrapolating from some small incident, or from a problem in an individual parish, and then presuming that it is the policy of the whole diocese.

What you should be most concerned about as regards the priesthood is the preparation you will receive in the seminary. It should be adequate spiritually and intellectually (Philosophy and Theology). Next you should know that as a priest you will be able to exercise your priesthood freely and according to the mind of the Church, with your bishop's support and in obedience to him. You should speak to the vocation director and the bishop about this.

This is a delicate point. Nobody is going to want to accept you if you are laying down conditions, because that is not what the priesthood is about, but I am sure that no one will object to your making a mature, reasoned and humble explanation of your concerns.

If you are still not at ease in your conscience with the answers you get, you might consider becoming a priest in another diocese. No matter where you go you will have plenty to do, and who knows what the future will hold. But serve without conditions other than communion with the Church.

---

what if I can't visit to see if I have a vocation?

Hi there. Just a quick question about discernment. I am currently looking into two cloistered convents. There is a local monastery that I frequent, and I do love being there. I love listening to the nuns chant the Divine Office and pretending I'm a part of it. (I also fantasize about being a mother of a huge 'good' Catholic family, so I'm not sure that this really means anything.) I often wish that there was some type of lengthened retreat in the monastery, so that I could just go and live with them and get a feel for their lifestyle, but that of course isn't the way it works. I find it hard to imagine selling everything and moving in as a postulant for a year, possibly to come back in another year to the same circumstances I'm in now. What do you suggest, in addition, of course to spiritual direction and prayer?

Dear Kaye,

The last two things you mention are the most important and helpful: spiritual direction and prayer. But, as you realize, they are not enough.

It's true that there is nothing like a live-in experience in a seminary or convent to really test your vocation, especially if you make it long enough for the initial novelty to wear off and give yourself the chance to experience the reality of the life you would be committing yourself to.

One of your fears seems to be that maybe your attraction to the contemplative life is purely emotional, you feel great when you are there to chant Office, but at the same time you realize that there is much more to convent life than that. And since you can fantasize just as easily about married life, you know that being able to imagine yourself there with the nuns is not enough to know you have a vocation. All of this tells me you are of pretty sound judgment.

If the convent rules do not allow you to live in for a while, don't worry. God is going to use some other means to lead you.

Your spiritual director and the convent vocation director will be able to tell you if they think it would be prudent for you to enter and test your vocation as a postulant. If they do, then the only really sure step you can take towards knowing if it is your calling is to try the postulancy.

It may not be necessary to sell everything in order to take the initial, one-year step. Perhaps you could leave your things in the care of someone you trust with indications of what to do if you are accepted into the novitiate or when you make your profession.

For now, while you look at this more closely in prayer, you could perhaps make some adjustments to your present lifestyle that will help you test yourself and also prepare yourself.

If you don't already have a fairly fixed daily routine, start now. Give set time to prayer, include Mass every day, rosary, spiritual reading, time for personal prayer before the Eucharist, go to the local convent regularly for Office. If you are used to working with background music, give it up for a while in order to experience silence (see how you work that one out with your roommate). This may mean cutting back on other things you like to do, but I think it will help you to live part of the reality of religious life before taking the step, voluntarily giving up of many normal and good things because God is asking something else of you.

This way you can test your resolve and your 'stick-to-it-iveness,' it will help you grow in intimacy and love with Christ, and you will be better prepared and know yourself better when the time comes to take a step.

CHAPTER EIGHT

Developing Your Vocation

CULTIVATING YOUR PRAYER LIFE

---

praying well

My question is that I pray every night to find my purpose in life and I have not gotten a response yet. Could it be because I am actually by some chance choosing the correct path?

Dear Rich,

Your whole point seems to be that you are in good dispositions, you even pray every night to find your purpose in life, yet the answer doesn't seem to come. This makes you wonder why: Is it because it is too late to be asking the question? Is it because the path you already are on is the correct one? Is it a question of your motivation?

I don't know the exact answer to this, but let me ask you a different question and then do some imagining: What kind of an answer are you expecting to your prayers? How do you think the answer is going to come to you?

At times we expect our prayers to be answered in the form of some unmistakable visible sign, like someone who does a novena to discover his vocation, and tells God to send him someone to give him an answer. Then, as soon as he finishes it, a perfect stranger asks him if he is going to be a priest. It is not good to look for this type of sign, because by doing so we are setting out conditions for God to fulfill. That's not the way it works.

God can of course send us a sign like this if he wants. But we shouldn't be counting on it, and much less stipulate it.

Other times we expect our prayers to be answered by an almost overwhelming interior illumination. We expect to be flooded with an absolute conviction in answer to our prayers so that we no longer have any doubt whatsoever about the path to follow.

This is not good either. It is too subjective. It begs the question: Couldn't this be just my imagination, some sudden euphoria? How can I be sure it really is God's answer?

So, how do we know what God is saying in answer to our prayers? Several things can help us:

One, remember what Jesus tells us, in essence: 'Your Father knows what you need even before you ask him for it. If he loves you, will he hold back anything that you need? You wouldn't do that to someone you love, and he loves you much more.'

Jesus also tells us how to pray, 'Seek first the Kingdom of God, and then you will receive all else as well.'

The important thing in prayer is not so much to ask, but to change. Often when we pray to find our way in life we say, 'Lord, tell me if it's A or B.' Then we don't seem to get a clear answer. It could be it really is C, or maybe even D. So to get our answer we have to change; we should not limit him to the choices we see, but tell him we are willing to do anything he wants us to do. When we start praying we are usually looking for what is good for us (of course, for all the right motives, but we are still looking out for ourselves). The outcome of prayer is that we begin to look out for what is best for his Kingdom.

As you pray better, certain convictions will take root in your life. You will be more sensitive to the needs of the Church and to the unique gift God gave us by giving us life; you will grow in the sense of how little this life can compare to the next, and how short life really is. All of this will affect your attitude towards the way you are going to live your life, and the choices you make. You will see God's hand and providence in your life more easily. You will have more of a 'sense' of what he wants you to do.

But it will never be absolutely clear. You will still need some prudent advice and direction from a spiritual director.

having a 'rule of life'

In a book I am reading it is suggested that as part of the discernment process one develop a 'Rule of Life.' This is defined as a daily, weekly, and monthly schedule in which you set aside specific times for prayer, study, work, meals, exercise, recreation, reading, and other priorities. Could you offer any advice as to how I would go about doing this?

Dear Danny,

The 'Rule of Life' is a very practical way of getting your life organized according to your priorities. You could say that it is just a religious name for time management which also takes into account your spiritual growth, and I would not limit its usefulness only to vocational discernment – it is a great way to get a handle on your life.

The handiest way to do it is to take pen to paper. Take a notebook you will use just for this and stick a few tabs giving a dozen or so pages to a tab. Mark them: priorities, problems, goals, getting there.

Under priorities list what is really important to you (character traits, qualities to develop, things you are going to do every day, the things you really want to do in each area of your life).

List also your problem areas. Your time-wasters (Internet, phone, TV), your weaknesses (such as inconstancy, impatience, vulnerability to peer pressure), the things you are sorry you did yet keep on doing. This takes time, and it will help if you keep a journal for a while.

Once you have done the above, you will need to state your goal. If you don't have a purpose (it is amazing how many of us have only a vague goal in life) you need to think it over. What type of a person do you want to be? What do you want to get out of life?

Now you need to make a list of the concrete things you need to do in order to achieve these goals in your daily occupations. For example, if you want to overcome laziness, you are going to have to go to bed and get up at regular times, you are going to have to make your bed each day. If you want to develop a prayer life you have to set time apart each day for prayer and devotions. If you want to know your faith you will have to take certain classes, or read certain books. The great thing about writing down these means is that it makes you be very clear and concrete.

Next you need to distribute your time between a daily routine and a weekly routine. Schedule in enough recreation.

I can only mention some general things here, but if you have someone who knows you that you trust, talk these things over with him in order to make this more concrete.

As regards your spiritual life, look at the goals you have set for yourself (for example: steady life of grace, openness to what God wants) and then the means (for example: more frequent confession, more personal discipline, more frequent Communion), and then see how you are going to fit each one in your day and week (when confession is available, time of day I can go to Mass, the prayer I need to do each day). Your friend can help you here to see you are not trying to do too much too soon, and that you are not doing too little too late, either.

Then look at your duties (studies, work, health, your obligations towards your parents), your goals and needs and how you spread them out over your week.

Then look at what you want to do for others (teach catechism, coach younger kids, lead boy scouts, instruct altar servers, help out with meals on wheels).

As regards your vocation, I would recommend that you gather the information you need, set time aside for a retreat, plan on visiting the places you are interested in, take care of obstacles (work to clear up your debts, for example), and look into the practical implications (when the entrance date is, what the application process involves). It is relatively simple to set deadlines on a calendar, and post it where you can see it.

It won't work out perfect the first time, but as you try it you will get to know yourself better and improve. Some people have more of a knack for organization than the rest of us. If you have a friend like that, get his help.

One final, very practical point: once you make a rule of life don't file it away. Stick it where you can check it at least once a day. I suggest somewhere not too visible because if it is always there you will end up not seeing it; it will no longer register even if it's there in front of you. Try the back of the door of a closet. Set a time (usually good first thing in the morning) to check on what you have to do today, and then another time (usually towards the night) to see how you did. You can include that in a short daily examination of conscience.

A SPIRITUAL DIRECTOR

---

how to choose one

How do we go about choosing a spiritual director? What are the characteristics that we should look for?

Dear Terry,

How can you find a spiritual director? Usually it is a safe bet to look for a priest.

He has to be someone you already trust, and, in your case, who loves and understands young people. Look for a priest whose preaching really reaches you (substantive, but practical and helpful), or one who spends a lot of time hearing confessions, or a chaplain in a school who does a lot of spiritual work with the kids (preaching, teaching, giving retreats, hearing confessions).

What you want is someone prudent and practical, balanced himself, and who has knowledge – although he doesn't need to be a genius. It usually helps if he is energetic and generally tends to be optimistic and unafraid of the truth.

A priest like this will most probably be busy, but in all likelihood he will find the time to help you if you and your group really want to work. Oh, and he must live close enough for you all to be able to meet up easily.

---

steps to find a director

In discerning my vocation, whether to consecrated or married life, I think it would be helpful to have a spiritual director. However, I've only been given a brief explanation of what one is and how to chose one. What should I consider when choosing a spiritual director? Are there any specific criteria (i.e. age, status in life) besides the obvious fact that they need to be faithful Catholics? Because I'm a woman, would it be better to have another woman as a spiritual director? Or our parish priest? What does having a spiritual director entail exactly? I'm a little confused but I think it would be helpful in discerning to have someone to vent all my ideas, prayers, thoughts, fears, and frustrations on, someone I could trust and be completely open with. The whole idea of discerning is so intimidating to me; I want to have someone to help me along the way.

Dear Anon:

The spiritual director does not have to be a priest. It is more common for him to be one, but it is not absolutely necessary.

The main quality to look for in a spiritual director is the gift of prudence, and a genuinely prudent person will always be both humble and strong. On top of that the director should have knowledge (both some learning and the gift). The spiritual director you choose, whether man or woman, should have those qualities. If you are looking for help to discern a vocation, the spiritual director should be a priest or a consecrated person.

Usually you come across a good spiritual director by reference—either through the recommendation of someone you know, or by hearing him preach, or by reading something he wrote—and that moves you to ask him.

In your present situation you may find it helpful first of all to go on a good retreat, preferably a silent one based on the Spiritual Exercises of St Ignatius, and as part of that retreat make a general confession. The confessor will be able to give you some initial advice as regards your vocation in the sacrament of confession, and may even be able to recommend a possible spiritual director to you.

At times we expect the spiritual director to do everything for us, do all the thinking and just tell us what we are to do. Normally he listens a lot more than he speaks to see what God is doing in your life, prodding you, making sure you are being honest, making you think and reflect, testing your conclusions. He will help you see the truth, but he will not make your decisions for you.

Don't forget as you do your search that 'your heavenly Father knows what you need even before you ask him.' So pray with trust and confidence for the right person to help you.

when I disagree with my spiritual director

When do you know when to move towards a vocation to the religious life and when it is better to stay where you are? I have been going to spiritual direction for a year and a half now. My spiritual director has told me that he doesn't think it is time for me to move on my vocation yet. At first, I was able to accept that, because I sort of knew that he was right. But for the past six months, this whole question of moving on my vocation has been coming up more and more. At first I think I was just being impatient. But now more and more my soul is telling me it is time. I am going to spiritual direction in a week, and I am going to tell him this. What do I do if he says no, it is still not time?

Dear Jamie,

It all depends on why your spiritual director thinks you should wait. As a general rule, if there is something concrete and important that you still need to work on before joining the seminary it is better to wait. If you are not perfect, but everything is 'normal,' then it is best to move – you can't wait until you're perfect before taking the step.

What are some examples of points that are advisable to work on before following your vocation? Well, if you are all fired up with thoughts of the vocation, but you are chronically irresponsible in your ordinary duties; if you still have some bad habit to overcome; if you have debts you have to pay off; if you are ill and need convalescence; if you have absolutely no control of your moods; if your prayer, vocation insight, and spiritual life are based on emotions only. All of this has of course to be taken in relation to your age. You would expect more of a college man thinking of the priesthood than a high school boy thinking of the minor seminary.

If you feel uneasy about what your spiritual director is advising you, ask him. Remember, the role of a spiritual director is not to tell you what to do 'no questions,' but to help you discover what God is asking of you so that you can understand, accept and do it. You have to actively participate in the spiritual direction and contribute your ideas and reflections. He needs to know what you perceive in prayer, what your inclinations are, what you honestly believe God is asking of you and why. His role is to shed light on these things, test them to see if they are valid and have the signs of coming from God, and let you know why if they aren't. He is trying to help you understand and follow the ways of God.

CONCLUSION

IN CONCLUSION

Again we are faced with the mystery of a vocation. It is in us—the fact that it is there is not our own doing—yet living it must necessarily be done by us, it is our greatest fulfillment, and also our surest death to ourselves; to respond freely we must be prepared to offer our freedom. Time and again the paradoxes return.

We can excuse ourselves in these paradoxes, or in our own impossibility of coming to mathematical certainty, both of the existence of the vocation and our ability to persevere in it, and bow out. The vocation is something we might like to entertain, but under other conditions.

What our difficulties often point to is the weakness of our own relationship with Christ, and the solution is not to be found so much in reasoning and researching about vocations as in getting on more familiar terms with him, through prayer.

I would like to end with this invitation: Pray. But don't pray telling God to send you a sign, or asking him to say more than he has already said in his Gospel. In your prayer ask him to make you more responsive to what he is already surely saying in your life. Ask him to help you be more generous. Offer yourself to him to do his work. Look at all the problems in the world around you; let them be Christ saying to you, 'I need you to do something.' And ask yourself what is the most you can do for him.

INDEX

INDEX